AFTER ALL THESE YEARS

AFTER ALL THESE YEARS
Our Story

foster & allen

with Anthony Galvin

2 4 6 8 10 9 7 5 3 1

First published in 2013 by Virgin Books, an imprint of Ebury Publishing

A Random House Group Company

Copyright © Mick Foster and Tony Allen 2013

Mick Foster and Tony Allen have asserted their right under the Copyright, Designs and Patents Act 1988 to be identified as the authors of this work.

All photographs courtesy of the authors unless otherwise stated.

Every reasonable effort has been made to contact copyright holders of material reproduced in this book. If any have inadvertently been overlooked, the publishers would be glad to hear from them and make good in future editions any errors or omissions brought to their attention.

Addresses for companies within The Random House Group Limited can be found at www.randomhouse.co.uk/offices.htm

The Random House Group Limited Reg. No. 954009

A CIP catalogue record for this book is available from the British Library

The Random House Group Limited supports the Forest Stewardship Council® (FSC®), the leading international forest-certification organisation. Our books carrying the FSC label are printed on FSC®-certified paper. FSC is the only forest-certification scheme supported by the leading environmental organisations, including Greenpeace. Our paper procurement policy can be found at www.randomhouse.co.uk/environment

Designed and typeset by K.DESIGN, Winscombe, Somerset
Printed and bound in the Great Britain by Clays Ltd, St Ives, PLC

Hardback ISBN: 9780753541937
Trade Paperback ISBN: 9780753555255

To buy books by your favourite authors and register for offers, visit www.randomhouse.co.uk

I would like to dedicate this book to all my family and friends who encouraged me, without exception, to follow my dream of playing music; and to the people of Milltown and Rathconrath, County Westmeath, for the great support that I have had from them, from my first concert there in December 1960 to the present day.

Also to Sister Agnes from the Convent of Mercy, Ballymahon, County Longford, who taught me the rudiments of reading music and who set me on the correct musical path; and to my great friend, Frank Gavigan of Rathconrath, County Westmeath, who taught me everything I know and love about Traditional Irish Music.

Without these two mentors, I wouldn't have had the successful career that I have today.

I will always be in their debt.

MICK FOSTER

I dedicate this book to my parents Patrick and Rose Allen, dearly loved and dearly missed.

TONY ALLEN

'Music that gentler on the spirit lies,
Than tired eyelids upon tired eyes.'

ALFRED, LORD TENNYSON

Contents

WAITING IN THE WINGS

MICK AND TONY

March, 1982. We stood still, taking it all in. Both of us were gripping our guitars, nervous under the heat of the lights. In front of us, two hundred cheering young people milled around and danced. To one side, on a different stage, a band was going through its paces. Directly across the studio from us The Boomtown Rats were standing there waiting, just like us.

We had been in the BBC studio all day, preparing for this moment. Now it was only seconds away. We composed ourselves, took a few deep breaths. We both knew how big this was. Even then we knew we would look back on this night as a defining moment in our career.

We had been on the road seven years together. We had toured all over Ireland and built up a bit of a following in the UK. We had been in America twice, and were finally making good money. The day jobs were a thing of the past. The dodgy vans and days of laying blocks and serving in hardware stores were over.

Our recordings were getting good airplay in Ireland, and 'A Bunch of Thyme' had hit number one a few years previously

– and again this year, when it had been reissued. We were on an upward arc, but how high we would go, or how long it would last, were questions only time would answer.

We were both in our green suits, frilly shirts and white socks – eighteenth-century Irish costumes we felt fitted well with our style of music. We both carried guitars, which was unusual. The accordion – a key part of our sound – was nowhere to be seen. We had been advised that it would not look right here, not on *Top of the Pops*. Then we saw Dexy's Midnight Runners standing on their stage with an accordion. We should have gone with our instincts!

But it was too late for that. The presenter, Bruno Brookes, stood in front of the camera in a flecked grey jumper. He smiled.

This was it.

He looked at the camera, and said: 'Here is a traditional song from Foster and Allen. They come from Westmeath in Ireland.'

And it was time to begin.

CHAPTER ONE

LIFE ON THE STUD FARM

MICK

Shakespeare once wrote of storms and earthquakes that shook the earth when Welsh rebel Owen Glendower was born. There were no such omens when I arrived, but it was bloody freezing. I was born in the black of the night on 6 December 1947, and my first few months were spent shivering against the cold.

It could have been worse; the previous winter had been the hardest on record, with six weeks of sub-zero temperatures, and snow all over Ballymore Eustace, my home place. Luckily, I missed all that.

I came into this world at Ardenode Stud, a little outside the village, and I was an only child for many years. So I was as familiar with horses as I was with other kids most of my childhood. My father was the horsebox driver for the stud, and he was also a ploughman, which meant I went to race meetings before I went to school.

My father drove the horses to the races. There would be two groomsmen or stable lads in the back keeping an eye on the two or three horses, and I'd be allowed travel in the back with them. God, it was mighty. I'd be allowed to hold the horses. If there was a problem with a horse we were meant to spot it and ring a bell in the back that would sound up front. My father would pull up, and we'd be able to sort it out. I was a brat of four or five, not even started school, and I was travelling around in the back of this truck with pedigree racehorses. I loved it.

Ardenode Stud was a fairly big affair in those days. It was owned by Captain Spencer Freeman. Captain Freeman had been around a bit – he was born in Wales in 1892 and educated in South Africa and New York. He fought in the trenches in the First World War, then settled in Ireland. In 1930 he was one of the founders of the Irish Sweepstakes, which raised millions for Irish hospitals. When the Second World War broke out he went to the UK to help the war effort, but he came home in 1946, and took over Ardenode Stud. He had a great interest in horses.

What made Ardenode an important stud was that it was close to Punchestown, one of the big racecourses in County Kildare. The annual Punchestown Festival, held every April, was a huge event back then. It was one of my favourite times of the year – and I still love it.

The races would take place from Tuesday to Thursday, but the previous Sunday was known as Walking Sunday. That was when all the jockeys and trainers would come to walk the course and check it out so that there would be no surprises when they were galloping it a few days later. Walking Sunday was great – you could see all these famous jockeys up close, people you had only read about in the papers. They were heroes to me.

And there were two races on Walking Sunday. Neither involved horses – they were cross-country races, a three-mile and a six-mile race for young lads. They would run the course that the horses would be on a few days later. It was fun seeing them struggle through the mud.

But it was even more fun coming back a few days later to see the horses run through the course. In Punchestown there were plenty of obstacles – the course had up-banks and drop-banks, and doubles and stonewalls, and all sorts of other treats for the horses to negotiate. So in Ardenode Stud there was a schooling ground, right at the back, with all those obstacles recreated.

We lived in one of the small houses attached to the stud, reserved for the staff. We didn't own the property – if my father lost his job, we were out on our ear. It was not uncommon back then. But what I loved about the house was that it backed onto the schooling ground. I used to sit on the paling watching the horses and jockeys running through their paces in preparation for the festival. That was a serious thrill.

At that age I just loved horses. I didn't know what a stud was, or why I was surrounded by the beautiful animals. But as I got older I understood the importance of the stud. They bred some great horses there, and did a bit of training – though that was a minor part of the business. Probably the most famous horse the stud bred was Ragusa. He won the Irish Derby, the St Leger, and the King George VI and Queen Elizabeth Stakes. But that was a lot later, in 1963.

The house we had was small – just two bedrooms. Back then there was no such thing as a 'good' room. Only the rich farmers had a parlour. We had a kitchen, where we spent our time, and a little room off it that my mother called the scullery. There were two bedrooms, and that was it. I remember the kitchen had a dresser with all the plates on it, and tins and ornaments. We had a big open fire with a crane over it. The crane could swing out and you'd put a pot or a kettle on it, then you would swing it back over the fire to boil water or cook. My mother would keep it on the boil for tea.

Ours was a kind of rambling house, where neighbours and friends were welcome to drop by every evening. People would be in playing cards and chatting. I was sent to bed, of course, but from my room I could hear the craic. Funnily enough, there was no music in my parents' house – they didn't even have a radio. In fact, we had little of the modern comforts we take for granted today.

My first big memory was when I was about five. My father bought a car. It was a second-hand Baby Ford, the smallest in the Ford range. That was sixty years ago, but I have never forgotten the registration number: IN 3584. That car was a serious thing to buy. We didn't even have running water in the house, we had no bathroom, and electricity was a distant dream. But we had our own car. Most working-class people were going around on bikes. Only the law-de-daws could afford a car.

I also remember going to Naas, the nearest big town, with my grandmother to do the shopping. We went in a pony and trap. It was only three or four miles, but in its own way it was as big a thrill as riding in my father's car. Those early years before school were brilliant – I was the centre of attention. There were just my parents, my grandparents (my father's parents) a few miles away, and the horses. Unfortunately my grandfather passed away when I was ten, but my granny was there throughout my childhood.

My father, Jack, was a quiet, placid man. I never saw him annoyed in his life. I have been told that if you got on the wrong side of him you might see a different man, but it took an awful lot to rise him. Years later, when I was driving, if someone cut in on us from a side road I'd be blowing the horn and cursing for Ireland. But he'd just tell me that I was wasting my time. If the driver had done wrong it was because he didn't know it. And all my blowing wouldn't educate him. That was my father's mentality.

My mother Jane was a different kettle of fish. She was fiery. If you got on the wrong side of her, she'd cut the legs from under you with a switch. And as there was only me in the house, it was me who got the legs cut on a regular basis! If I acted the hoor, God help me. She ran the house. She looked after everything and she was a great organiser. I remember that she had a number of tins that she kept on the dresser, one tin for each bill. There was a tin for the insurance man, a tin for the butcher or grocer, a tin for each one of them.

One of the tins was for what we called the Jew Man. It sounds horrible now, but that is what we called him. He mightn't have been a Jew at all, but our one was. He was a draper who operated on credit. He'd come around with his wares and you could buy a suit of clothes, a pair of shoes, or a dress, and pay it off over the next few weeks or months. My mother dealt with him, and with all the others. She kept those four or five tins on the dresser, with a few shillings in each one of them, so she never fell behind on the bills.

Once a week we'd go into Ballymore Eustace to do the shopping. It was a substantial village, with a population of a couple of hundred. My mother made the two-mile trip on a bicycle, coming home with all the groceries in a basket in the front, or on the carrier at the back. Sometimes I'd be on the carrier. It must have been luxury to her when we got the Baby Ford.

The car had no heating or luxuries like that. In the winter you'd be dying of the cold, and the windscreen would fog up something terrible. On long trips we would have rugs and hot-water bottles to keep us warm. But then my father got his hands on a great device: the demister. I have no idea where he got it, but it plugged into the battery in the engine with two wires, and it had suckers to stick it to the glass. It didn't give us any heat, but at least the windscreen didn't freeze any more.

Christmas was a special time. We would spend it with my maternal grandmother in Moneygall. Every year we would all bundle into that car, with our rugs and our flasks of hot drinks, for the long trip to her place. Moneygall is a tiny village on the Offaly/Tipperary border, famous for producing the great-great-grandfather of American President Barack Obama. It was a sixty-mile trip, and the Baby Ford chugged along at thirty miles an hour. So it was an epic journey, two hours of bumps, draughts and chills. Just like the house, there was no radio in the car.

We'd arrive on Christmas Eve and stay until St Stephen's Day. I enjoyed the craic, but there was something even more important: I got two Santas. He had to come to me at my granny's, and my main present would be waiting for me when I got home to Ballymore Eustace.

I don't remember my maternal grandfather, because I was only eleven months old when he died. But my granny was always there, and my mother's sister and her husband. And there was my father, my mother and myself. I suppose I was doted on to an extent, being the only child among so many adults. But that didn't mean I'd be let get away with anything. Back then you didn't give cheek to adults – you knew your place. I didn't dare step out of line. If I was told not to do something, I wouldn't even consider doing it. In that era, you were afraid of everyone. You were afraid of your own parents, you were afraid of everyone else's parents. And you were afraid of priests and nuns and bishops and schoolteachers. If you saw a policeman coming you'd nearly get into a ditch the other side of the road.

Maybe as a young lad that registered, because up until the age of seven, I wanted nothing else but to be a Garda. I had grand-uncles in the police and often saw them coming and going in their uniforms. I wanted to be a detective, but I had to be a Garda first. But when the time came I was too small for the Gardai. And then they let down the height restriction, but I was still too small. Finally they got rid of the height restriction, but by that stage I was too old! In any case, by then music was for me.

But back to Christmas: as an only child I didn't have to share with anyone, and that was a blessing. My Moneygall granny – that's what I called her – played the concertina and accordion, and she had a brother who played the concert flute, and another who was an All-Ireland step-dancing champion. So there was music and craic in that house every Christmas.

It might have been my Moneygall granny, Johanna Meaghar, who introduced me to music, but it could just as easily have been my Ballymore Eustace granny, Mary Kelly, my father's mother. She loved music too. I began to listen to the music in both my grannies' houses. My Ballymore Eustace granny had lads in regularly who would play music in her kitchen. They were just neighbours, having a bit of fun. Such visits were common in rural Ireland in the days before television. We had to make our own entertainment. While some would play an instrument, other lads would be singing. I was over there on a regular basis, especially once I hit about seven and got my first bike. As I got a bit older and began to go to school, my visits became a regular part of my week, and my love of music grew.

I was music mad from as long as I can remember. It ran in a broad vein through the entire family. A cousin of my father, Chris Connolly, played with the Gallowglass Ceili Band from Kildare. In the fifties they were one of the best known ceili bands touring the country. They had a commercial edge that the Tulla Ceili Band and the Kilfenora didn't. It wasn't pure trad, but people loved them. They travelled all over the place, even as far afield as England and Scotland. They also toured America.

The Gallowglass was the first music I was exposed to. They were playing in a big marquee in Poulaphouca, a tiny village up the mountains from us. I was only about seven at the time, and there wasn't a hope that I would be let in for the ceili, even with my parents. But my father wanted me to at least get a sample of the fun.

I remember him lifting me up and sitting me on his shoulders. He stepped inside the marquee for a few minutes to let me see the boys playing on the stage. They had two accordions, a fiddle, a piano, bass and drums. And there was a guy with a saxophone, coming in and out of the music.

The marquee was stuffed. There were hundreds of people jammed inside. I didn't see how they could dance, there were so many of them.

And the sound just washed over me.

I never wanted to do anything else from then on – only play music.

CHAPTER TWO

A MUSICAL FAMILY

TONY

I suppose I am as Irish as you can get – I was born within shouting distance of the very centre of the country. The river Shannon – the biggest river in the British Isles – almost splits the country in two as it flows from County Fermanagh in Northern Ireland down to Limerick on the south-west coast. It separates my native Westmeath from Roscommon.

Just north of Athlone is Lough Ree, the second largest lake on the Shannon. And that is where you find the exact centre of the country. It is just to the west of a little island in the middle of the lake, Cribby Island. If you ran from my house for twenty minutes across the fields and through the hedges, you could get to that lake, and within a stone's throw of that little island. So I was born that close to the middle of the country.

I came into the world on 24 February 1952, into a house already bursting at the seams. I was the youngest of nine children. My parents were both from the parish of Mount Temple, and that is where I grew up, the son of a farmer in a vibrant community. Mount Temple is a small place, but with a

21

rich history dating back to the time of St Patrick. The village lies between Athlone and Moate, but off the main road. There is a distinctive church modelled on the Church of St Teresa in Avila, Spain, a school, a pub, a shop, and a population of just five hundred, but that hides the real story. Like many similar small towns and villages in Ireland, there is a great community spirit that always makes me proud to belong there. Even today as I drive along the road towards my childhood home after a long tour abroad, when I get to my own little patch of Ireland my eyes might mist over. There is a certain spot on the road, after which I am back where I belong. My wife Trionagh says she can actually see the change come over my face.

Today Mount Temple might be best known for a very good golf course – a new addition since my childhood. We lived a few miles out of the village. My father farmed forty-two acres, with the help of the nine of us. He also worked for the county council.

My father, Patrick, was an only child, but he did not remain alone for long, because he met, fell in love with, and married my mother Rose Doyle, and they raised a large family together. He must have been swamped in the house, but he loved it. In contrast, my mother had many brothers and sisters and took it all in her stride.

They christened me James Anthony Allen, but I was always known as Tony. That kept things simple, because there was another Anthony Allen in the village, and he was around my age. In fact, we went to school together, and it could have led to confusion. But he was known as Anthony, and it was never shortened. We were cousins but, surprisingly, we were related through our mothers rather than our fathers. Our mothers were first cousins. There were also two other James Allens in the parish, but they were a lot older than me. Perhaps we lacked a bit of imagination when it came to choosing names!

Living on a farm dominated my childhood. Depending on the season we all mucked in, doing whatever needed to be done on the land. It was the same with all our neighbours: when work beckoned it was all hands on deck. Country living has its charms, but it could also be hard work. Despite this, or perhaps because of it, I had a very happy childhood.

The farm wasn't a big one. My grandfather, Michael Allen, had been a herder for the Hudson estate that crossed a lot of the countryside nearby. But the estate had been divided up by the Land Commission in the early years of the century. The Commission tried to rationalise all the tiny, divided farms that were a relic of the famine and the land wars. Some farmers could have three or four parcels of land separated by a few miles, which were a nightmare to tend. The Commission rejigged things and tidied up the situation. So at least our farm was one piece of land. My father, as an only child, inherited the whole thing from his father. And the house I was raised in, a few miles from Mount Temple, came with the land.

The house was a small thatched one, with no running water. It nestled behind a grove of trees, which in theory protected us from the worst of the weather. All the things we take for granted today, such as electricity and indoor plumbing, were still a long way in the future.

The land supported us after a fashion. We kept a few animals and grew some vegetables. But on its own it wasn't enough. It was subsistence, not a living. So my father worked for Westmeath County Council as a carter. Carters were the men who manned the horse and carts for the council, transporting stuff and doing odd jobs. I remember every morning he'd be up at seven, and he'd head off down the road with the horse and cart. He'd come back around seven in the evening, tired from putting in a long day. A typical day might see him filling the cart with gravel, then spending the next several hours going around the small country roads filling in the potholes. Mile after mile of bad road would be made passable through his efforts.

With the state of our country roads now we need a return to those days. Patrick Allen would be a hero today!

When he'd come home and have his dinner, he might have to go out again afterwards and do the farm work. But it wasn't too hard on him. He was awfully lucky that he had nine children to help out. We all had our chores to do, and we did them willingly enough. And as the youngest I seemed to inherit more and more of those chores as my older siblings left home.

My father was a quiet, kind man, and very easy-going. He didn't say a whole lot, but what he said, he meant. He was wise, and had a great knack for reading people. There was a sense of calm about him. To this day you would struggle to find anyone with a bad word to say about Patrick Allen. Because my father was so easy-going, he got on well with everyone. I think – I hope – I inherited some of his qualities.

He played a bit of music, too. He was a nice fiddle-player. In his earlier days he played fiddle with the ceili band in the village. They would have trotted out all the traditional favourites. But with nine children, a day job and a farm, I suppose the fiddle had to take a back seat, and by the time I arrived it was only something he played around the house when people were in.

I missed out on all that earlier fun. There was a little hall outside the village called the Duck House. In his younger days he played there once a fortnight, with some of his friends and musicians from around the village and the surrounding area. But if he liked his music, there was one thing he hated: dancing. I never saw him dance. I never remember him – even at weddings or functions – being a dancing man. He loved playing music, and he loved going to functions. But he never took part in the dancing. I suppose I inherited that too. I'll get up and play all night, but do not ask me to take to the floor!

My mother was a total contrast in many ways. She was a lively woman who loved the craic, and she could talk for Ireland. She loved telling stories and listening to them, and the sound of her laughter filled the house. She was at the centre of every bit of fun, while my father sat on the periphery with a smile, enjoying it all in his own, quieter way. They were the perfect foil for one another. She was always singing around the kitchen, or humming away to herself as she did her daily work. I take after her in that. My wife says I must be the only man in the world who can sing one song while an entirely different song is playing on the radio behind me.

Another memory I have of my mother is of the smells in the kitchen as she prepared our dinner in the evening. She'd be pottering about, humming a tune as she bent over the stove, the aroma of boiling vegetables, roasting meat or freshly baked bread permeating the air, and battling with the more acrid pungency of the tobacco smoke drifting from my father's cigarette. I knew which smell I preferred – perhaps it is one reason why I was never tempted to smoke myself.

My mother wasn't quite as easy-going as my father, but she was a great woman to help people. Her kindness, to me and to others, is my abiding memory of her. She was the warm heart of our home for the nine of us.

My brother Mick was the eldest, a full seventeen years older than me. He was already a man when I arrived as a wee baby. When I hit seventeen it struck me that he was already thirty-four, twice my age. I'll always remember that.

He was followed in order by the four girls. There were Margaret, Brigit, Mary and Anne. But we never called Brigit by her given name. She was always Beasie to us. After the four girls, it was back to boys again. Jack and Pat and Tom came ahead of me. Tom was two when I was born. He was closest to me in age, and I suppose we were thrown into each other's company for that reason. And he shared my love of music. In fact, under the name TR Dallas, he became a big star in Ireland with a number of hits. We played in the same band for a while.

But Tom and I weren't the only ones. All of the family were musical, each in their own way. Whatever they were into, or however their lives turned out, music played its part.

I don't remember Mick growing up, because when I was just three he emigrated to England. I have no memory of him leaving, which will tell you how young I was. But I do remember the great excitement there was every year when he would return to visit. We were delighted to see him, of course. But at that age I was just as excited to see what he had in his bag. He always returned with some goodies for us – maybe a leather football, or some new toy that was all the rage in England. And records – plenty of them over the years. And I have fond memories of him returning twenty years later, to settle in Athlone with his wife Maisie and their young family. It was funny to think that his kids were closer to me in age than he was.

Mick played the pipes, and the accordion, and he loved to sing. And football was a great interest of his. He played a lot over in England. The four girls were also interested in music. Anne, the youngest, was a lovely singer. Give her half a chance and she will still jump into a session and break into song. Her three daughters, Annette, Moira and Rosaleen, are the same way. Rosaleen, the youngest, is in a successful band in Birmingham now.

Mary, like Mick, emigrated to England, ending up in Birmingham with her husband Michael O'Connor and her son Philip. It was always such a pleasure to visit her when we were touring the UK. Like my mother she was a great talker, and always looking for news. There would be a million questions whenever we met her – every little bit of gossip had to be passed on. Like many emigrants she knew everything that was happening at home, down to the smallest detail. And she often knew it before I did! A large part of her heart had remained in Mount Temple, and for that reason she had more of an interest in home affairs than those of us who remained at home, and

took things for granted. I always got a great welcome from her
– a gas woman.

Jack, the second eldest of the boys, was more into football than
anything else. In fact, he played well into his forties. But he
loved his music – as well, and was part of a successful band called
Jack Allen and Allendale. Back in the eighties and nineties he
gigged a lot around Ireland, but he also had his own business as
a mechanic, and a growing family, so the music had to be
relegated to second place. He never lost his love of it though.
And all his family inherited the voice. His daughters Jackie,
Michelle, Roisin and Anita, and his sons Sean and Paul, can
be heard singing in the choir every Sunday at our church in
Mount Temple.

Pat, the next in age, had more interest in the land than any of
the rest of us. In fact he is still there with his wife Mary, but the
house is a lot more modern now. He keeps the farm going still.
As a youngster he played the fiddle. And he'd have a session
with anyone who would come around. He and Mary had three
children: Padraig, Tina and Margaurite. Pat and his wife still
live in the home place to this day. It is such a warm inviting
house. I could walk in and before I would get a chance to sit
down Mary would have a fry on the table for me. And Beasie
and Margaret drop by the whole time, just as if my parents were
still alive. Because of the sort of people Pat and Mary are, it is
still the 'home place' to all of us.

The second youngest was Tom, or TR as everyone knows him
now. Tom was never interested in instruments. For him it was
always singing. He wanted to be up front, belting out the songs.
And he achieved his ambition. He's made a good career out of
Country and Irish music. He became one of the biggest stars in
the country, on the back of a very clever hit. There was a
television programme that ran from the late seventies through
the eighties called *Dallas*. It was set in the world of the super-rich
Texas oilmen. One of the leading characters was JR Ewing, who

was shot at the end of one series. For the rest of the year, until the series returned, there was only one question on everyone's lips: who shot JR?

Tom recorded a song which told this story, released in 1980 – 'Who Shot JR Ewing?' He got a big Stetson hat, changed his name to TR Dallas, and the rest is history. The song was a huge hit, and he followed it with 'It's Hard to be Humble', a very funny song, the same year. 'Daddy's Girl' was another of his hits. In our younger days – before we both achieved success – we often played in the same bands.

That was the roll call in our house. With so many into music you'd think that times like Christmas would be a virtual concert, but not so. For one thing, Mick and Mary and Anne had emigrated to England, so they were gone. And then Margaret married. I only barely remember her in the house when I was very small. But she married locally so she was always part of my childhood. I have great memories of calling on her and her husband, Pat Joe Hughes. What I remember more than anything is that she baked the best brown bread in the world. I defy anyone to find better. Warm from the oven and lathered with jam, it was a great treat. I was always very close to her children. I still am great friends with them all: Father PJ (a priest currently on missionary work), Kathleen, Margaret, Bernadette, Marie, Frankie and Jim.

It's funny not to have any memories of the four eldest at home during my childhood. It is a bit strange to come from a large family, and yet in a sense not come from a large family, if you see what I mean. But I don't think any large family would all be at home together though. They couldn't be. And we had only a small house with a couple of rooms, primitive plumbing, and no electricity in my early years. So where would we have put everyone?

The house had a thatched roof and was sheltered from the worst of the weather by a row of trees that broke up the wind in winter. Today you would call it quaint, but back then we envied the townies with their slate roofs that needed no maintenance.

With so much emigration in Ireland, a lot of families became reluctantly estranged from each other because of the distances involved. Back then, it took a whole day and a night to get to England – and that was only if you had the price of the fare! In that respect I was blessed with my chosen career, as it allowed me to see so much more of my family than I otherwise would have. But I was luckier than that, thanks in part to the music. In my late teens and twenties, when I was touring in England with various bands, I met up with my brothers and sisters over there. It was one of the perks of touring, a bonus to be able to call in on them and enjoy some home comforts far from home. Our first stop when we arrived in the UK would always be at Anne's house in Birmingham, where she lived with her husband Aiden. We'd take the ferry over, arriving in Holyhead in the small hours, then drive through the dawn, arriving at Anne's house in time for breakfast. We would all sit around the table – us tired after a long drive, and her young girls lively and ready for school.

After a breakfast full of laughter and news she would bundle the girls off to school, and we would slip upstairs and take their beds to catch a few hours of much-needed sleep. It was a most pleasant way to start our tour. Mick and Mary also lived in Birmingham, and we might catch up with them when we woke up, or we would see them at one of our shows.

Of all my sisters, Beasie is the one I remember best, because she stayed home until she married, and she married locally. I remember her courting her man, Robert Greene. Everyone called him Bunny, and I had great time for him. I would have known him as well or better than I knew my own oldest brother. And as with Margaret's children, I get on very well with Beasie's kids: Ann, Rosemary, Bridget, Seamus and Patrick.

In those early years, before I began primary school at six, the house and farm were my entire world. I remember my father sowed some vegetables, and kept some cattle. There were always a few pigs, and a couple of cows to supply milk for ourselves. He had about three cows, which he milked daily. And every day, after taking out our own supply, he'd sell half a can of that milk to the Mount Temple Creamery. It mightn't have seemed much, but at the end of every month it would come back to us in a cheque that made a fair difference to our household budget.

We grew our own potatoes, turnips and carrots. And we kept chickens and ducks. The taste of a freshly laid egg boiled for the breakfast beats anything you get today. And we'd keep a turkey for Christmas. That was quite common – lots of country people did. We would fatten up the turkey over the autumn, allowing him to roam free near the house. Then, a few days before Christmas, he would meet his fate – a quick blow of the axe, then he'd be plucked for the table. That was a big job, and would keep my mother busy a whole evening.

A neighbour of ours, Joe Seery, had a hackney car. A car was a rarity back then, and it was one of the few in the district. The same man had a tractor, with a mowing arm, and a plough, and a threshing machine. My father would work with him every year. Come threshing time the two of them would travel from farm to farm, for however long it would take to thresh the whole parish, and maybe two or three neighbouring parishes.

That would be mid- or late summer, because I remember we were at home from school a lot of the time. And if we weren't home, we'd get a day off for the threshing. We'd follow the thresher to six or seven houses, which was great. At every house you'd be given tea and cake, and maybe ham sandwiches as well. Everyone would muck in at the work. If you have never lived in the country, and never joined in a neighbourly day of threshing, bailing or hay-saving, then you cannot understand the sheer sense of fun involved in those days. Everyone was in it together.

There would be chat and gossip while we worked, and during the breaks we would sit down in the field under the bright sun, mugs of tea in hand, and set the world to rights. At least, the adults did. We ran around like it was our own adventure playground.

Years later, John Duggan, a good friend of ours, wrote a song about those days called 'The Old Threshing Mill', which we recorded. Every time Mick sings it in a concert I am transported back through the years. For three perfect minutes I can relive the memories of those halcyon days: the hard work in the field and the dinner afterwards – bacon and cabbage, and butter-drenched spuds. As the song says, 'it makes a man hungry, the old threshing mill'.

My father also worked with a man at the ploughing. He had the horse that he used for the council carting (which he had to supply himself). And the other man had a draught horse. They'd harness both horses to the plough for the coring. This was what they called opening the drills. They'd start with my father's farm, then they would do the other man's. Then they might do a few of the neighbours' farms.

For a while my father had his own horse-drawn mower, which he would hire out to the neighbours. He'd mow their fields, and the few pounds would come in very handy for us. That was in my older brothers' time. My arrival coincided with the introduction of tractors into the parish, and that side of my father's activities swiftly dwindled. Tractors eliminated a lot of the old ways, but they did make life a lot simpler. A fellow would come in with a tractor and mow the meadow on his own, and it was all done in half the time.

The old was being swept away, and I remember when modernisation came to our own house. We got rid of the thatch, and replaced it with a slated roof. That was a big change for us. We were moving into the twentieth century. But we placed no value on what we were abandoning in the name of progress.

Today we would fight tooth and nail to hold on to the thatch. Then it was just a symbol of the poverty of the past.

Changing the roof was a very big job, and not something that was done lightly. But fate played a hand. There was a small bit of a field in front of the house, and we used to call it the Grove, because it was thick with trees. And those trees were thick with crows. There were endless crows, cawing away day and night. You'd hear the racket all the time. But one night there was a huge storm, and in the morning a lot of the trees had been blown down. Our thatch had taken a beating. We were faced with the decision of redoing the thatch, or putting in what we thought of as a 'proper' roof. Practicality won out.

Some of our neighbours were skilled tradesmen, and we got them in to do the work. Some men had to put in the wooden beams and rafters to support the roof, then others would climb up and lay the dark thin slates in neat rows, nailing them to the wooden framework. I remember looking up and over a few days seeing the bare ribs of the house gradually being fleshed with sleek black slates. We thought it was a great modernisation.

A few of the houses around us were what we called Land Commission houses. You could always tell them, because they were properly built, maybe even having a tiled as opposed to a slated roof. And they would have had toilets out the back, in a little outhouse. We were edging closer to the luxury represented by the Land Commission houses. We had the roof now; all we were lacking was the bathroom.

And as I've mentioned before, in those early days we had no running water. Often I would see my father going out in the winter, early in the morning, and smashing the ice on the barrel under the eaves of the house. He would scoop out a basin of the freezing water, and come back into the kitchen to wash his face and shave. You wouldn't do it today.

I was nearing the end of my time in primary school before they rectified that problem. A number of years after we got the new roof, we built a small extension out the back. They built on a bathroom and another room. Now we had electricity and plumbing. We were living in the lap of luxury.

CHAPTER THREE

MY GRANNY'S GRAMOPHONE

MICK

I was five or six when I picked up a musical instrument for the first time. There were always tin whistles and mouth organs lying around. They were cheap instruments, and always in tune, so everyone had one. There was an old melodeon – a type of accordion – in my granny's house, and I began playing with that as well. It was messing about of the highest order at that stage – no rhythm and no tune. But it was a start.

Around the time I began to mess with the instruments, another big change came in my life – I began school. I went to the local national school, which was in the village. It was a two-mile trip every day, but I didn't have to make it on my own. There was a fellow whose father was a farrier in the stud, and he used to come across the fields and pick me up in the morning. He was a few years older than me. I was about six, and he was eleven or twelve. He'd take me by the hand and we'd go to school.

There were five teachers. Mrs Gallagher taught the infants, juniors and first class, so she was my first teacher. Her class was mixed, boys and girls. But when you stuck out your chest and got to second class, it was boys only. For the next two years we were in the tender care of Miss Hayden. In fourth class we were taught by Mr Gallagher, our junior teacher's husband. And there were Mrs Woulfe and Mrs Doran, who taught the older girls.

It was a segregated school for all the older kids: boys kept apart from girls. And it was total segregation, despite the fact that we shared the same building. There were separate lunch times and break times. Once you passed first class you couldn't get near the girls, which was a persecution. But I made up for that after!

I loved school. I had a small brain but I never had any trouble there at all. That was back in the days of corporal punishment, but I got off very lightly. I only got two slaps in all my years at school. And I put in for both of them. If I got ten slaps the same day I couldn't have complained. I think it happened when I was in second class. By that stage I was up in Miss Hayden's class. She was an old woman, not long from retirement, and I suppose she did not have full control of the class. We were acting the maggot all the time.

One day she got really mad, and she came down and began beating the head off one of the boys. I thought he wasn't getting enough of a beating, so I joined in and began hitting him too. She was beating him, and I was beating him. But I didn't realise there was a glass partition over the door, and we could be seen. The principal, Mr Gallagher, had a full view of the whole thing. The first I knew of that was when the ominous tap came on the window. The master came into the room and he was in a towering temper. He slapped me twice, once on each hand. And the slaps lifted me out of it. I never forgot it.

I was about two years into school – seven years old – when I got my first bicycle. There were cut knees and shins and elbows for a few weeks. I'd get into a speed wobble, and down I'd go. But eventually I got the hang of it. Once I was good on the two wheels I had a bit of independence. I was able to go to school on my own without my hand being held, and I was able to cycle to my grandmother's after school a few days a week. I'd have my supper there, and later on my mum and dad would come over in the Baby Ford. They'd be there for a couple of hours, then they would throw the bike in the back of the car and we'd drive home. I loved the sense of independence, of being able to wobble around the parish on my two wheels.

It was in my granny's house that I really got to hear music. My parents were into music a bit. My mother could knock a tune out of a melodeon or a mouth organ, and so could my father. But they were never musicians as such. Neither was my granny. She didn't play any instrument at all. But there were often people dropping by who would belt out a tune or a song. And she also had an old gramophone, and a world of 78s, the heavy ceramic records from the pre-vinyl era. She had Jimmy Shand, a Scottish accordion player, and traditional players of all sorts.

This was back in the days before electricity, so you had to wind the gramophone up. I remember that one of the springs was broken, so it didn't work properly. The only way you could get music out of it was to put your finger in beside the little spindle in the middle, and spin the record like crazy. Lord, you'd have great music, but you had to get the timing right. And I was young and my finger got tired easily... It would begin as sweet music, but before long the jigs would become old-time waltzes.

It was flawed but it was enough to give me a love of music – that and the impromptu sessions in the kitchen with my granny's guests.

I loved the school holidays because we often went to Moneygall, and I could be there a couple of weeks. My other granny was a musician, and so were many of her family. My cousin Tony Maher was a few months older than me, and he was really into the music. I'd be running around playing cowboys, and he'd be there playing his music. I was beginning to mess around on instruments, and I used to watch him and dream of some day being as good as him. He went on to play in a showband, the Conquerors, out of Galway.

But it wasn't all music, on holiday or at home. Ballymore Eustace was famous for handball players. Not the Olympic handball, but the Irish version. It is the very same as squash, except that you fist the ball against the wall. It's a sport I loved from the beginning. I started around the time I began school. There have been times in my life that I have not got the chance to play as regularly as I would like, but it has never gone from my life. I still play at least once a week. But now I am playing against fellows my own age, because I have slowed down a bit! We meet religiously every Thursday night in Mullingar, and play for an hour to an hour and a half. It keeps me ticking over.

I was six or seven when I became involved for the first time. And I never improved. When you start something, whether it is music or sport or any skill, after three to six months you are a lot better than the guys who never started. Unfortunately I have never progressed beyond that six-month plateau, despite a lifetime of devotion. I never became any better. I would beat the hell out of a lad that had never played, but my big problem – then and now – was that I couldn't keep my eye on the ball. At the last second I'd look into the corner where I was going to bury the shot, and then the ball was liable to go anywhere.

I also boxed for a good few years. I began in the local club in Ballymore Eustace when I was about ten, where I learned all my basic skills. I was a lot better at the boxing than the handball. Indeed, when I was twenty, I became the Westmeath Featherweight Champion. But I never boxed in the Leinsters, or took it any further. As I got better at the boxing I was also improving at the music, and I knew which one had priority. My thumb began to hurt after fights, and I had to stop. But the boxing genes live on. I have two lovely grandchildren, Sarah and Daniel, and Daniel took up boxing. I am proud to say he became Irish and British Universities Champion, as well as Connacht Champion.

But although I was sporty, I never played football, beyond a kick-about with my friends as a boy, and I certainly never tried hurling. Lads ask me why, and if I am honest, it is because I am too cowardly. In the boxing the lads in the ring know the rules, and we abide by them. No one is going to try and kill you. But in hurling or football a lad can come up behind you and bury you before you know a thing about it!

It's ironic, because there is a great history of hurling in my family. A forebear of mine, Ned Meagher, played for Tipperary against Galway in the first ever All-Ireland hurling final, played in Birr in 1888. He was on the winning side. And in 1961 my cousin Matt Hassett captained the Tipperary side that beat Dublin by one point in the All-Ireland final.

It was a normal childhood and I had plenty of friends in the school, and to play with after school. One of my best friends was Pat O'Connor. We did everything together. Then, when he was about twelve, his family moved to Kerry. It was a terrible wrench – I haven't laid eyes on him since. Pat, if you ever read this book, make sure to get in touch!

Though music and sport and school friends were important during my childhood, what stands out more than anything is the gradual encroachment of the twentieth century on rural Ireland. One of the big things I remember was the beginning of modernisation in the village. When I was young we didn't have a toilet inside. We had a shed outside. And it wasn't a flush toilet. It was an Elsan Dry Toilet, and my father had to dig a hole and bury the waste every week. It sounds prehistoric now, and I suppose it was – a little shed, like you'd see in a cowboy film. But a lot of homes didn't even have that. They just had the forty-acre field.

We didn't have running water either. Everyone used a well or a pump. We had a well down the field, and my father would bring up the water for cooking. And there was a barrel in the yard to catch rainwater for washing. Of course, there was no electricity.

The running water arrived when I was about eight. It felt like real progress, to be able to get into a bath. Before that I'd be put standing in a steel basin in front of the fire, and my mother would wash me from head to toe on a Saturday night. She'd have me shining like a snot on a hob going to mass on Sunday morning.

When the water came – and the toilet and bathroom with it – our world was turned upside down. Then the electricity came too, and we never looked back. We had our car, and lights, and water. What more did we want?

But things were changing. Captain Freeman gave up the stud, and the new owner was a shipping magnate who spent most of his time in Hong Kong. Jim Mullion took over, and he brought big changes. A new trainer, Paddy Prendergast, began working with the horses, and the stud became more commercial and more successful.

There were other changes too. My father was no longer the horsebox driver. I don't know whether it was a promotion or a demotion, but he became the chauffeur for the Mullions when they were home. And they weren't home often. They spent half the year in the Far East. He got paid for the full year, whether they were there or not – so it was a great job in that sense. And, as it would turn out, he was needed more and more at home.

For it was around that time that my mother began to weaken. She was suffering from multiple sclerosis, a degenerative condition. It began with muscle spasms and weakness, and over the years it become progressively worse until she was bedridden. The early signs were there while I was still in primary school, but at that stage she was still able to lead a normal enough life. Over the years she steadily declined.

But change wasn't done with us yet. In 1960, my father lost his good job. I am not sure of the details, but I think there was an argument with the stud manager while the Mullions were in Hong Kong, and he quit. He managed to get a new job in Westmeath, again as a chauffeur. But the whole family had to move. Like my friend Pat a few months previously, I was leaving Ballymore Eustace for good. My regular jaunts over to my granny's to listen to the gramophone were over.

CHAPTER FOUR

THE LURE OF THE GUITAR

TONY

Like most fellows I started school around six. I went to Mount Temple National School, which was a four-room building. There was a small room for the infants, first and second class, and a bigger room for second to sixth class, with two teachers. This was repeated on the other side of the building for the girls.

Although the boys and girls were in the same building, it wasn't a mixed school. It was two separate schools sharing the same physical space. There was a wall in the middle of the building, extending out to the road, like a semi-detached house. And it was more than your life was worth to cross that wall. Boys and girls did not mix, not even during the breaks. We could see them over the wall, but we could not play with them.

The school was three miles from my house, and I walked to and from there every day. There were a few children up the road, and if I came out of my house and walked down a by-road and across a field, I would meet up with them. We'd walk across the fields and cut to the road, from where we could get to the school. The field we crossed is now a golf club.

There were only a few cars in the area at the time. If you were lucky someone would be driving down the road and they would give you a lift to school. I was down a quiet road, and there would only be a few children, so there was a good chance of the lift. Other kids lived down busier roads. There could be six or seven of them in a bunch, and they never got lifts.

I never enjoyed school, perhaps because I was not very academic. Ours was a small school, with four teachers. A woman taught the younger kids, while a man took the older classes. It was the same on the girls' side of the fence. My first teacher was all right. But when I moved up to the big boys, I was worried. Now I was going to be taught by the master we had previously been sent to if we had been bold boys in the junior class. He was the disciplinarian who kept us all in order – I had grounds to be worried! But when I got up there, it wasn't as bad as I feared at all, as is often the way with childhood troubles.

When I was about eight I got a bicycle, I don't know from where. My brother Jack was a mechanic up in Moate, and he had a car. He would take me and the bicycle up to the school every morning, on his way into work. I would cycle home in the evening. That made an awful difference – life was suddenly a lot easier. At that time people thought nothing of tossing a bike into the back of a car. We wouldn't do it now.

Looking back on it I don't remember the bad weather, but this is Ireland so there must have been plenty. I can't remember getting wet on the cycle home, but I do remember the tar on the road melting in the summer heat, and how the tyres of my bike would stick to the road, making the cycle tougher than it should have been.

Getting the bike broadened my horizons. Now it was easy to cycle up to the village after school and find someone to kick a ball with. It was easier to meet up with friends and to feel part of the bigger world. There was a green area in the village and I was always sure to find a few lads playing football.

Football was my passion back then, and it still is. My wife wouldn't call it a passion; she'd say obsession. She jokes that there should be a clause in the marriage contract making football addiction grounds for divorce!

Every fine evening in my childhood we would all head out to the village on our bikes. There was a little park there, which we called the football pitch, and we would toss out a ball and play for the evening. Most of it was Gaelic football, but we occasionally played a bit of soccer as well. During the good months that would have happened five or six times a week. I played for the parish team too, until I left school and began gigging regularly. Then the music interfered with the training, and one had to go. But I never lost my love for the game, and every Sunday, if I am not on tour, I will try to catch a local game. My local team is Caulry, and I will watch them in anything: senior, junior, under twelves, under sixteens, minor, I don't care. I will be on the side cheering them on. And I follow my county, Westmeath, almost as fanatically.

I remember once, years later, returning from a tour of Australia. I was gone for four or five weeks and returned home late on Sunday night. At eight the following morning, my phone rang.

'That's my alarm call,' I told Trionagh. Then I jumped out of bed and drove from Lurgan, in Northern Ireland, down to Thurles in Tipperary – 180 miles away – to watch a game. Jet-lag be damned: I had to support the boys. But there was picture and no sound in our house for a week!

As a lad, football was more important to me than music. But growing up in the sort of house I did, a love of music was never far away. My parents had what we called a rambling house, which I loved. On a Saturday night Ceili House was on the radio. Not every house had a radio, but we did. So people would drop by to listen. My brother Pat played the fiddle, and so did my father. So with the music on the radio and the music in the kitchen, it could be great craic. Any Saturday or Sunday night, and maybe one or two nights during the week, there could be six or seven people in our house, chatting and listening to the tunes.

We lived in a little loop off the main road. On the loop there was one married couple with no kids, two bachelors living together, a man and a woman in the next house, again childless, then a couple with just two kids. One house had four bachelors living alone. There was some amount of bachelors living in our area! A lot of them would ramble into our house on Saturday or Sunday and listen to the radio, and stay talking until maybe two in the morning. Sometimes there would be a bit of a session. I didn't play at those impromptu sessions. I shouldn't even have been awake. But I was. I was listening, enjoying the craic. Perhaps more seeds were being sown as I listened to the music and the effect it had on the neighbours.

It would begin with Ceili House on the radio, then a couple of fellows would begin playing. Another thing I remember from those evenings is that my brother Pat was a handy man with the shears. He was only about nineteen or twenty at that stage, but he would cut all the neighbours' hair. People would sit down on one of the kitchen chairs, while the chat flowed around them, and he would snip and trim. He didn't do it for money. It was just a neighbourly thing.

I began my musical career on the button accordion, when I was eight or nine. But I never got very far with it. The instrument was not for me. I was interested in contemporary stuff. I also liked folk music. And I wanted to be able to sing, like Johnny McEvoy.

But the button accordion did at least get me started. There were classes after school once a week, given by Willie Reynolds. Willie was well known locally as a musician, and a few of us kids would go up to the school in the evening for the classes. We learned a few tunes and got to play together. It sparked an interest in me.

My brother Tom only ever wanted to sing, whereas I saw myself as a musician. I wanted to strum a guitar like the guys I heard on the radio. At school, whenever the teacher would give Tom the chance, he'd be up on his feet and singing. I was never asked, and I never volunteered. I didn't start singing for a number of years. I never had any interest in feiseanna or fleadhs or any of the opportunities in the trad world. I just wanted to play the guitar and be part of a group.

My chance came when I was about twelve. A friend of mine down the road from me, John Buckley, had an acoustic guitar. I don't know where he got it – it was a strange thing for anyone to have back then. He was knocking out tunes on that, then he moved on to an electric guitar. So my mother bought the acoustic guitar from him for me. It was not a typical instrument for a young lad, at least in Ireland, and perhaps it was an indulgence we could ill afford. But my mother must have seen some spark of talent in me. Or maybe she was fed up of listening to me strangle the button accordion. Little did she know what she had started. It was only a cheap guitar, but it got me through my first few years. Now I am a proud owner of a Lowden, a beautifully crafted guitar made in Northern Ireland. Lots of famous musicians and singer/ songwriters choose this one, so I feel I am in good company.

Around the same time there were some big changes in the parish, which also pushed me in a musical direction. The changes began towards the end of my years in primary school. It was decided that the parish needed a new and more modern school and over a number of months, we watched the new building going up. Finally, around 1963, the new building was ready. It was officially opened, and we moved in. By then I was twelve, and had only a year or so of school left. But it was a vast improvement on the old school. For a start, the days of separation from the girls were over. Now we had a mixed school. And there were more rooms, and running water, and toilets that were properly plumbed. The school even had cloakrooms.

But there was an even more important change. Along with the new school came a new teacher. He had one thing in common with the old master – they were both called Ryan. My, he was a breath of fresh air. He brought new energy and enthusiasm to the school. Dan Ryan transformed the whole place. He was a modern teacher with a whole different attitude to the kids. He treated us with respect, and in turn we respected him. He organised a bus tour for us, and a sports day for the village. He also organised drama, which was great. Up until then those of us with an interest in music or drama had no outlet. All of a sudden there were dramas at Lent. Lent was still big in those days. In the forty days before Easter we would cleanse our souls by giving up sweets or other childish indulgences. The build-up to Easter was as big as Easter itself, and the Lenten dramas were part of that. During the interval you could get up and sing a few songs, or play a bit of music with some other lads. I loved it. Who knows – maybe standing there in front of all my mates, singing a song and holding their attention, planted a seed in my mind that would blossom into a career?

From the beginning I felt comfortable on a stage. I *belonged* there.

The new master also interested us in algebra, which I loved. Oh, he changed everything. He broke down the divide between pupil and teacher, but he was no pushover. He was a great teacher with a knack for getting us engaged and interested. Even years after, if you bumped into him in a pub, he was great craic, and full of interest in you. You could sit down and have a laugh with him, and he was genuinely interested in how you were doing. I have very fond memories of Master Ryan.

A little later we got a new priest, Father Jimmy Byrne, and he changed the parish as well. He interacted very well with people, and the older people loved him. He became part of the parish, rather than a standoffish figure at the top.

Although I enjoyed my childhood, one of the things I didn't like about growing up was that I was always made to be a messenger boy. All the old bachelor fellows felt they could drop into our house and sit down for a chat, and while they'd be there, they would ask my mother to send me up to the shop for them. The shop was only a mile up the road, but by the time you got back, that was two miles. I did it because that is what we did back then. But if I had a legitimate excuse to make myself scarce, I would take it!

There was plenty to keep me occupied. When I got home from school every evening there was no shortage of chores to keep me busy. Pat had an interest in the farm, but we couldn't leave it all to him, because he was away on a building site working all day. So I'd go to the well and bring home a couple of buckets of water. In the right season my father would hire someone to dig up the potatoes. But otherwise it was my job to go out to the field and bag those potatoes and carry them home.

The cows had to be brought in every day too, of course. All of us had to do those jobs, but being the last I saw my brothers and sisters leaving the nest – and leaving more and more of the work to me. My friends were in the same boat. We had a stoic attitude about it: we all helped out, because the work needed to be done. That was life back then. And there was time over afterwards to kick a football or mess on my guitar.

And then we got electricity, which was another great change. With the electricity came the television, and that was another distraction. It could be addictive. In the evening I just wanted to sit down and watch the box. I didn't want to run around the fields after cattle, or drudge through the drizzle to the shop – though of course I never said no. My older brothers and sisters didn't have that distraction to contend with.

Soon, *Top of the Pops* became my weekly fix. Tom and I would sit and watch it every week, and in the schoolyard the following day it was all we would talk about. We both loved music.

I still find television a wonderful tool for relaxation, particularly when I am on tour. In a strange hotel room, with time to kill before or after a show, it is great to flick to a rerun of one of my favourite comedies. I love the oldies – *Last of the Summer Wine, Open All Hours, Only Fools and Horses*. I am not the greatest man for sleeping, and if I find myself restless I will always be able to find something to sit down and vegetate before. Old habits die hard.

With the electricity came other joys, too. My sister Anne was working in England, and when she came home on a visit one time, she brought a record player with her. She left us a few Elvis records, and a Clancy Brothers LP. Oh, I played them until I almost wore them out. A whole new world of music opened up for me.

And the world itself was widening too. At the age of thirteen, a year into the new school with the new master, I sat the primary cert, and luckily I passed it. It was time to move on. I had enjoyed my final year in primary school. The new building and the new master helped enormously. But I was happy that I was now going to secondary school in nearby Moate. It was about six miles away, but I could leave the bike behind. There was a school bus to bring me there every day, and back again in the evenings to face the chores. Another milestone had passed: I was out of short trousers and into my teens.

CHAPTER FIVE

A CHILD AT THE MICROPHONE

MICK

I was twelve, with a year to go still in primary school, when our little family was completely disrupted, and transplanted to County Westmeath in the centre of Ireland. My father was lucky enough to get a new job as a chauffeur, and again it was a cushy enough one. He was now driving for Lady Lister-Kaye, so we were moving up in the world.

Lady Lister-Kaye was a French-Canadian aristocrat, and her Irish base was Mearescourt House near Rathconrath, a little spot in the middle of nowhere between Mullingar and Ballymahon. Mearescourt House was an impressive Georgian pile built in 1760. A long avenue of lime trees led to the three-storey mansion, which had ten bedrooms, and was set in hundreds of acres of its own grounds.

We weren't in the main house, of course, we lived in a house in the yard. Downstairs there was a kitchen and a bedroom, and upstairs there were two more bedrooms and a bathroom. It wasn't any bigger than what we had left behind, but it was spread over two stories. It was a converted stable, and it had plumbing and electricity. We were used to such luxuries by now.

It was also very handy for my father. All he had to do was open the door and step out, and he was at work. And Lady Lister-Kaye was like the Mullions, in that she spent half the year out of the country. He had fallen on his feet.

It was a wrench leaving Ballymore Eustace in May 1960, and I missed my old school friends and old haunts. But, being young, it didn't take me too long to make new friends. I started at Miltown National School within a few days of arriving in Rathconrath, and I loved it there. It was only a two-room school, which was a comedown from what I was used to. Ms Casey was our teacher – she took all the classes from second upwards.

One of the reasons I loved the school was that it was mixed. It wasn't big enough to be segregated. And a lot of the kids came to school in their bare feet, particularly in the summer. At the top of the class there was a small pot-bellied stove to keep us all warm. In Ballymore Eustace we had central heating, so while at home we had moved up, at school I was definitely moving down in the world. The younger kids sat up front, so they got the benefit of the stove. We older kids sat at the back, and on a cold day it could be like a Siberian Gulag.

We had our lunch in school, and many of the kids brought a bottle of milk or tea to drink. We would put all the bottles around the stove at the start of the morning to heat them up for lunchtime. There was a popular cure for indigestion at the time, milk of magnesia, and it came in a very distinctive deep blue bottle, around the size of a hip flask. It was the right size to fit in a lunchbox, so was a popular choice. Every day there would be a few of those by the stove. But you had to be careful: as the bottle heated up, the pressure would build. So you had to unscrew the top a bit, to let the steam off. Sometimes a kid would forget, and there would be an almighty explosion: the bottle had burst and milk would blow to the clouds.

Another memory I have of that school was that every second Sunday they held a fundraising ceili in the school. Eventually, they built a new school on the proceeds of those ceilis. There was a small stage at the back of our room, where the band would perform. And on Friday afternoons, as soon as the bell rang, the older kids had to clear the classroom for the dancing. We would move the desks back, and take down the maps and charts from the walls.

Of course we weren't allowed to go to the ceilis. We were too young. But they made an exception for me, because I was beginning to play, so they knew I was there for more than the craic. I wasn't good enough to participate, but I loved listening to the band. I'd be at the ceili on Sunday night in my long trousers, and on Monday I would be back in the classroom in my short ones. There were no other young lads there. The next youngest to me would have been seventeen.

I only did about fifteen months in that school before moving up to secondary school, but they were fifteen very enjoyable months. I was beginning to find my footing in the local music scene, and in the parish as a whole. We had two priests in the parish. The Parish Priest was Father Brady, and the curate was Father Kerley. Father Brady was not a great man for early mornings. Getting up on time was a problem for him. On Sunday morning there were two masses, one at eight thirty, and the second at eleven. I was an altar boy, and I got used to both men's rhythms. If I knew that Father Brady was saying the early mass, I knew it might not begin until ten to nine. So if I got there at quarter to nine, that was grand.

But sometimes I would get it wrong, and Father Kerley would be doing the early mass. I'd arrive, and find the mass nearly over!

Father Brady was no better at getting up during the week. But he had to say mass every morning. Often we would be doing our lessons, and I'd hear the roar of his car coming flying up the untarred road towards the school. I'd hear the tyres crunching on the gravel, and I'd smile to myself, but I'd say nothing. Next moment Father Brady would come running in, looking for someone to serve mass. I was the senior altar boy, as I was near enough the oldest. So I'd be nominated.

I'd hop into the car with him, and off we'd go to the church. Often enough the church was empty – no one there but the priest and me. After the mass he'd tell me to hang on, and he'd give me a lift back to school. But it was less than half a mile, so I never took him up on the offer. I'd walk back. I'd set a good brisk pace ... that would see me not make it back until just minutes before the lunch break.

More than once I made it back for the lunch break, had my lunch, and he'd be back again, looking for some young lads to move a cow from one field to another, or some other odd job. It's a wonder I got any education at all.

Before leaving Ballymore Eustace I had sat the Primary Cert. I didn't think I had got it, so the following year I sat it again in Milltown. I passed it – then discovered I had passed it the previous year as well. So I passed the primary cert twice. I was thirteen and it seemed high time to move on to secondary school, taking my double certification with me.

The secondary school was in Ballymahon, a good eight and a half miles away from my home. The school was a convent, run by nuns. It had been all girls, but two years prior to my arrival they began admitting boys. So there were no boys in the upper classes, but a few of us in second and third year. There were five of us in first year, and there were forty girls. So it was eight to one. Lord, it was great.

I did the distance every morning on a bad bicycle. It was a seventeen-mile round trip. But it wasn't so bad – there were guys further away than me who were doing nineteen miles a day. I had no belly on me, and I was as fit as a fiddle, despite the fact that I wasn't playing handball any more – the club was too far away.

There was a club in Mullingar, which was twelve miles distant. But it might as well have been in Botswana for all the good it did me. Mullingar was the nearest boxing club as well, so I had to give up that too – until I hit seventeen and had my own car.

So I was reduced to kicking around a football with the lads, which wasn't my thing at all. The sports I enjoyed were individual ones. I suppose I grew up an only child, and I was still an only child as I prepared for the new school. But that was about to change.

My mother's condition was deteriorating as I began secondary school. It was as if the move to Westmeath marked a turn for the worse. Back in Ballymore Eustace, I remember noticing that one of her hands and arms had no power in it and one of her hands kept closing on its own. A condition like MS creeps up on a person slowly. As she deteriorated we became used to her new limitations, and accepted them as a fact of our life.

When we moved my mother was pregnant. My parents must have been tremendously excited at this development. Large families were the norm in Ireland back then, and they must have been really looking forward to the new addition. But by the time little Patricia finally made her appearance, the pregnancy and the move had taken their toll on my mother. She had declined badly. It very quickly became obvious that she was not strong enough to mind a new baby. It must have been a heartbreaking decision, but Patricia was sent back to Ballymore Eustace, where she was raised by my grandmother and my aunt.

Looking back, it is hard to know how I felt about that. Patricia arrived screaming and bawling, and suddenly she was gone. I never had a chance to build up a bond with her, so having her so far away was a lot easier on me than it was on my parents.

But though she was far away, she was not out of our lives. For the next number of years there was a weekly or fortnightly pilgrimage in the Baby Ford over the sixty miles to see her. Although we saw her regularly, we were missing all the landmarks: the first smile, the first step, the first word. Since I had been an only child all through my formative years I didn't appreciate what I was missing. But now that I have kids and grandkids of my own I can see that it must have been torture on my parents, especially for my mother, to have had a daughter and to have had to give her away.

I am thankful that Patricia and I developed a good relationship as adults.

My mother wasn't completely weak at that stage, but it progressed rapidly. She couldn't do anything. Soon she had to be lifted wherever she was going. As her condition deteriorated she had to be fed and washed and brought to the toilet. Before long it was very bad. If my father was away working it fell on me to feed her and bring her to the toilet. Looking back now I suppose it was tough on me. But it was something that had to be done, and I didn't think about it. I knew the other lads my age had parents who were flying around the place, but I didn't give it much thought. I did what had to be done, no big deal.

My father's job was great when Lady Lister-Kaye was in Canada. But when she was home he could be gone for the whole day. And if she went out for dinner that evening, he could be back out again and not home until twelve or one in the morning. I was on duty then. I went to school, did my homework, practised my music and looked after my mother. That was it.

I was getting serious about the music. Back in Kildare I had started messing on a button accordion, and when we made the move that instrument made the move with us. But there was no one teaching me at that stage. I was doing my best on my own. In Westmeath I switched to the more expensive and complicated, but less traditional, piano accordion. I don't know why I made the switch, but I did. And I was three months rooting and rasping at that instrument when I had a stroke of luck. The world of traditional music is a small and tight community. Eventually you get to know everyone, and everyone gets to know you. The shared interest brings you together. I got to know Frank Gavigan from Rathconrath. Frank was a button accordion player, and a great musician – he had won the All-Ireland back in 1952. He took me under his wing, teaching me how to play properly.

My first public performance came when I was thirteen. It was in Milltown National School, at one of their fundraisers. It wasn't one of the fortnightly ceilis, but a more serious event altogether, the annual Christmas concert. This was held every year in the school as a fundraiser, and there was a bumper raffle. There must have been a hundred prizes, and the night would go on for ever. It was a concert, featuring a number of local acts, and I performed solo, which should have been daunting for a newcomer, but wasn't. I remember playing 'Tipperary So Far Away' on the button accordion. Although I was in the process of switching to the piano accordion by then, I stuck to the more familiar button accordion for that concert. And I steered clear of reels and jigs – I wasn't ready for them yet. But I played one or two simple tunes. It was mighty to be on stage, and for a while I was a sort of celebrity with the other young lads.

My mentor Frank Gavigan was a number of years older than me, and steeped in the music. I found him an inspiration. I would watch him listening to a tune on the radio, and he would be able to write it down as it was playing. Sometimes I would be pestering him to teach me a tune. He might be in the pub enjoying a pint and a cigarette. He would hastily scribble the notes on the back of the cigarette pack, and hand it to me, then go back to his pint. So of course that got me interested in learning to read music.

Coming under Frank's tutelage had an unexpected bonus. The button accordion is more traditional than the piano accordion, and I was trad mad. Being taught by a button player, I picked up those mannerisms, despite playing a different instrument. So I was playing the piano accordion like it was a button accordion, and no one had ever played it like that. I am not saying I was better than other lads, but I sounded different. And people recognised the difference – my playing began to stand out.

I approached one of the nuns in the school, Sister Agnes, and asked her for her help. She was a piano teacher, and had not worked with an accordion, but she was willing to take on the challenge. She also taught me to read music.

So I was getting my trad from Frank and a grounding in music from Sister Agnes. It was a good combination. When people heard me, until they saw me they thought I was on a button accordion. And at that time, in the trad world, piano accordion was a dirty word. The old guys hated the new instrument but I was somehow able to bridge that prejudice. What I was playing sounded so different from what they expected; they thought I was the greatest thing since sliced bread. With the result I went on to win three All-Irelands.

The All-Ireland's were a big deal in the trad world, and they still are. For those who didn't grow up with it, the key events in the trad world are the Feis Cheoils and Fleadh Cheoils, which both translate to festivals of music. The feiseanna were musical competitions held annually in various towns, such as Cork and Dublin. The fleadhs were organised by Comhaltas Ceoltoiri Eireann (The Society of Musicians of Ireland). Comhaltas is the primary organisation in Ireland promoting traditional music, song, and the language. The regional Fleadhs staged competitions in various categories, and the winners went on to the All-Ireland championships, held in a different town each year.

They have a bewildering array of categories – tin whistle, flute, fiddle, war pipes, mouth organ, whistling – you name it, they seem to have a category for it. I specialised in the piano accordion. I began to play in all the fleadhs and feiseanna around the midlands, building up my experience. There were age categories, so I was competing against lads of similar experience, or lack of it.

Performing in a fleadh is an odd experience. It is all done without fuss or fanfare. Your name is announced by an impassive MC, and you walk on to the stage. Facing you is an audience composed of your fellow competitors and their parents, and a table with a panel of judges. You play your piece as purely as you can – no hamming it up for the audience – then you walk off and await the adjudication. Not for everyone, but I loved it. I never felt it as pressure.

I was fifteen when I won the Leinster championship for the first time. That gave me a real thrill. It was a sort of rite of passage. Now I was a real player, not just some young lad rasping away on his instrument. Winning gave me status within the traditional world, and gave me the right – and the confidence – to mix with the players I had admired from a distance. The following year I won the Junior All-Ireland, and in 1968 and 1970 I won the senior All-Ireland. But that is jumping the gun.

I didn't have a touch of nerves playing – then or ever. But Lord, I knew before I ever walked onto a stage for the first time that this was what I wanted from my life, if I was ever good enough. And I instinctively knew that being good was not enough; you had to be well known to get the gigs. I understood that from the beginning, which is why I pushed myself in competitions once my skills improved, and why I pushed myself to get a chance to broadcast my music.

Back then there wasn't the plethora of local radio stations and satellite television stations that there is today. Radio Telefís Éireann, the national broadcaster, was the only game in town. With a monopoly you'd think it would be difficult to get on the airwaves, but all it took was persistence. There were programmes that showcased emerging talent.

A friend of mine, Raymond Smith, was a button accordion player who had already performed on the radio. He told me how to go about getting on. I followed his lead. I was fifteen and coming off my win in the Leinster championships when I wrote to the Controller of Programs at RTÉ and asked for an audition for one of their programmes, *Children at the Microphone*. I knew they held them around the country. Eventually a letter arrived telling me there was a place reserved for me at an audition in Athlone. My father bundled me into the Baby Ford, and off we went.

It was in a local hotel, and there was a panel of three adjudicators in a small room. The three of them were behind a table, and I was called in and sat on the opposite side of the table from them. But I wasn't daunted. By that stage I was well used to playing in competitions, so I was used to being judged. I was convinced I would do a great job. I was brimming with confidence. It was fierce important to me that I got to broadcast, so there was no way I was going to screw this up.

Despite my confidence there was a tense six-week wait before I got the word back that my audition had been successful, and I was to play on *Children at the Microphone*. I would be broadcasting from the GPO in Henry Street, the RTÉ headquarters in the centre of Dublin. On the appointed day my father acted as my chauffeur once more, dropping me to the door at the right time.

The presenter was Pat Laide, an actor from Mullingar. I knew him slightly, and his brother better, and that helped. The arrogance of youth also helped. There were about six of us sitting in a circle around the upstairs studio, and there was a big hoor of a microphone hanging down in the dead centre of the room. Pat would call us up to the microphone one at a time, and you would say your name, and where you were from. He might ask you a question or two, then you were on. You would play your selection, then retreat to the periphery again while the next hopeful came up to the microphone. It was going out live, so if you screwed up there was no going back!

Then you would sit there quietly while Mary or Johnny or Brigid did her bit, and on around the circle until it came to your turn again. We all got two blasts of this, and I was delighted with myself. To me this was it: I was broadcasting. The radio was the big thing back then; this was 1963, and we had only got the television two years earlier. So if you got on the radio you were a minor celebrity.

All my classmates were tuned in, and my music teachers. At school the next day I had to talk about the whole experience. The teachers were all over me, and so were those who were into the music. It was great for the school, and great for Sister Agnes. Then the next day it had all been forgotten about, and it was back to normal, as if it had never happened. But then I would be cycling home in the evening, and there'd be old lads who had played a bit of music, and they'd all want to stop me and have a chat. They'd tell me how good I was, and how they loved the tunes I had played. They delayed me so long I was late home, and I was starving! These poor old devils were praising me and being nice to me, and I was lapping it up, as any young lad would. But by the end I'd be thinking, couldn't some of you wait until tomorrow and let me home to have my dinner?

Between the ages of fifteen and seventeen I was very lucky in that I managed to get on the radio quite a bit. Once you got on first, it was easier after that. They knew you, and knew you would not let them down. I appeared on *Children at the Microphone* about four times a year, and every time it was the same: I got my fifteen minutes of fame, at least around Westmeath. Shortly after my first radio appearance I also got on television for the first time, on a show presented by traditional player Seamus Ennis. He is best remembered for his recommendation that the best way to play a bodhran is with a penknife! He was an uilleann pipe player, and the show was *Seamus Ennis sa Chathoir* (Seamus Ennis in the Chair). It was a television version of *Children at the Microphone*, and you had to be under seventeen. It was a strictly all trad show, which suited me.

It was a bit daunting to be in a television studio for the first time. I was surprised at the heat, caused by all the big lights. And the cameras were huge. The zoom apparatus was not as sophisticated as it is now, so the cameras had to move in and out a lot more. You'd be playing away and the cameraman would be across the room. The next thing the hoor would come flying at you, and you'd be wondering if he was going to stop at all, or was he planning on killing you and breaking your accordion? But once you got used to that you passed no heed, except for the heat.

Side by side with my music, I still had to go to school every day. My minor celebrity status didn't change any of that. Though I wasn't academic I loved school, and it suited me grand to sit there with my friends, and chat and mess about during the breaks. But music wasn't what we chatted about in the yard, because my interests were narrower than those of most of my friends. I listened to nothing but traditional music growing up. The Beatles and the Stones might as well have been chanting monks for all I cared. By my teens I wouldn't even listen to the Gallowglass Ceili Band or Jimmy Shand any more. It had to be pure hardcore trad. And if someone had asked me to play an old-time waltz I would have been insulted. It was reels, jigs and hornpipes – or nothing.

Music became my all-consuming passion. Every chance I got I would go to the local hall and listen to the ceili bands. I was well able to dance, but I wouldn't bother my arse. I'd just listen to the music and study the players, and imagine myself up there playing with them. After I won the Leinster championships I began to get a bit known among the local musicians, which expanded my horizons. New players taught me new tunes. I made new friends through the feiseanna and fleadhs, friends who shared my obsession. Among those new friends were Denis and Cecilia Ryan from Edenderry, about half an hour away from my home.

Every weekend for about three years I would head off to Edenderry on Friday after school, and I would stay with the Ryans until Sunday. A couple of years older than me, Denis was a great fiddle player, and we used to play a lot together, so I would go down to his house. His sister Cecilia was an All-Ireland piano champion. They were near enough my own age, and as cracked about the music as I was. We travelled regularly to fleadhs together, so it made sense to go there for the weekend. My parents didn't mind – they knew how important the music was to me, and I was beginning to have a little bit of success. The broadcasts had also made them a bit famous locally. All their friends and neighbours would be talking about seeing me on the television or hearing me on the radio. In truth, it was probably a break for my mother as well, as her health continued to decline.

I learned a lot from Denis. We still play together regularly in pub sessions and at trad events. The way he'd teach me was simple. He'd play six notes of a tune, and I would play them back to him. Then he'd play another six, and I'd repeat those. Then he would play all twelve, and I had to do the same. I'd pick up a new tune in five minutes. I learned the world of tunes from him.

Sometimes I'd practise two hours a day, sometimes three. My parents would bring me up to Frank Gavigan twice or three times a week, and I could be there from eight o'clock until after midnight. How did I ever find time for study?

I was still working away at school. I did three years in the convent, and sat my Inter Cert, a state exam you sit when you are about sixteen. The Inter Cert is still important, but back then it was very important, as many people did not remain in school for the Leaving Cert or go on to third level. So for most of the country the Inter Cert was our final exam, and our success determined our employability to an extent.

I was never a great scholar, and I suppose I was distracted by the music. Two weeks before the Inter, when all my classmates were cramming their heads at the books, I travelled up to Clones for the All-Ireland Fleadh Ceoil, where I won the Junior All-Ireland. I came back from that on a high, and had to bend my mind to maths. Maths was a key subject – fail that or fail Irish, and you failed the entire exam. Not only was I no good at maths, it was taught through Irish. This was a huge disadvantage to me, because I wouldn't recognise my own name over a shop door in Irish, with the result that I learned nothing.

My parents weren't too concerned. They were still over the moon about the music, particularly my mother. She could be exacting when it came to that. If I was learning a tune in the kitchen she would send me off to the bathroom. It was the furthest away room. I'd have to go up the stairs and down to the end of the corridor.

'Go up there and practise,' she'd say. 'And don't bother coming back down until you can play it.'

I could leave the accordion upstairs and come back down, but I wouldn't dream of bringing the accordion back down and rasping into her ear. It had to be right, or the instrument couldn't come into the room. That made me take my practice seriously. She always said that if you could hum a song you could play it, and I have found her theory to be fairly right. I am lucky in that I can learn by ear, or I can take a sheet of music and read it and play it. Most musicians have to play by ear.

Funnily enough I don't ever remember her being as exacting about the study!

And, unsurprisingly, studying didn't feature much in my final year at school. I was too busy with the music. I also got a regular gig. There was what we called a practice ceili in Loughnavally, about eight miles away on the road to Athlone. A practice ceili was where people would come to learn how to do all the traditional dances. A band would play and some experienced dancers would help them through the steps.

The practice ceilis were held every Tuesday night, and a banjo and mandolin player called Billy Whelan was responsible for the music. Billy was the most famous musician in Westmeath at the time. He was also broadcasting, and unlike me it was on the adult talent shows. I came to his notice, and he asked me to join in with him. It was like playing with God – he was a superstar to me. Billy would get a pound for the ceili, and I would get ten shillings. I was fifteen when that started, and still at school.

I remember it was five shillings to get into the ceili in Milltown. The ceilis came around every fortnight, and I was getting ten shillings every week. Even someone with my mathematical skills could do the sums. I would have a pound in my pocket. Even after paying for the price of the dance, I had money over so I could chat up a young one, and buy her a mineral or whatever. I could stick out my chest. I had money in my pocket when other lads my age had nothing.

But I was still in school, and could not put off my exams. I eventually had to sit the Inter. And maths was the problem I expected it to be. I got by all right in the other subjects. I had a good grasp of history and geography. I was good at commerce. But I scraped by in arithmetic and geometry, and flunked algebra entirely, and my average was below the pass mark. So I failed the entire Inter Cert.

I can't even remember exactly how I did. And it didn't matter a jot. I was still on a high after becoming All-Ireland champion. There was a photograph of me in the local paper, and a write-up. I was a star – what did I care for exams?

Enjoyable though school had been, for me it was finished. If I couldn't pass my Inter Cert, what was the point in hanging on for the Leaving Cert?

My school days were over.

CHAPTER SIX

TECH DAYS AND MARQUEE NIGHTS

TONY

Leaving the security of my beloved Mount Temple – and the new school with the new master that had made my final year so much more enjoyable than the years that went before – was a big step, but I was ready for it. There was no secondary school in the village, so I had to go further afield.

There were three secondary schools in Moate. There was the tech, the Convent of Mercy and the Carmelites. The Convent of Mercy was all girls, so that ruled me out. The Carmelites was a boarding and day school for boys who had an academic leaning. The tech was for people who wanted to learn a trade. It seemed a safe choice for me – I knew I was never going to be an academic high flyer.

Secondary school was a big change. It was a mixed school, like my primary school had been for the final year. And it felt like a natural progression, so I adjusted quickly. It helped that football was big in the school. I had a try out for the school team for the county championships. I made the team a few times. But it wasn't a big deal to make the county team at my school. We were definitely second string compared to the Carmelites. They had a far stronger team – all the good footballers went there. They won three or four schools All-Irelands in that time. We had our own good footballers, but it was not as exciting as playing for the Carmelites. Still, it was good craic.

I was also able to hang out with lads who were into music like I was. A couple of the lads were playing music. At that stage I was only playing the guitar. I had dropped the button accordion, and I haven't played one since. My brother Mick had brought the accordion home from England for me, but I put it aside for years, and finally I gave it to my nephew Padraig, who is a professional musician in America now.

I wasn't great on the guitar, but the attraction was that it had more scope as an instrument. You could sing and play along on the guitar. Occasionally I played with lads in the school, just for fun. Two of the lads I played with were Johnny Bastic, who played guitar, and Josie Adamson, who played both the accordion and the keyboard.

I regularly went back to my old school in Mount Temple for dances, and also to the neighbouring Drumraney National School. I took any opportunity to listen to live music. They had fortnightly sessions as fundraisers, and they had their own resident dance band. They were called The Marylanders, after the local Maryland Football Club. While I was still in secondary school my parents would let me go out in the evening and attend the dance. The school hall was just down the road so there was never any danger. There was no bar or anything, so it was safe for a teenager to go along.

As teenagers we had to mingle with the older people at those dances; there was no place else to go.

I still remember my first public performance. I joined The Marylanders for a few songs at the Drumraney dance. It was the regular Friday night fund-raiser. John Buckley – who wasn't in the band – was there that day with the electric guitar he had got after selling his old acoustic one to my mother for me. John had no intention of playing, and I don't know why he brought the guitar along. Maybe he was going somewhere else afterwards. But the band were easy-going, and when they saw him with his electric guitar slung over his shoulder, they invited him to come onto the stage and join in for a few numbers. He did, but after a few minutes John decided he wanted to dance, so he left the instrument down and took to the floor. I stepped out from the crowd and picked it up and played a few numbers with the three boys.

It was absolutely brilliant getting in front of a crowd for the first time. It was thrilling, and I loved it. I had no nerves at all. There were two accordion players, Paddy Moran and Dick Brown, and a drummer, Johnny Moran, that night, as well as myself. It was great craic. They were playing the big country hits of the day, songs like 'Lovely Leitrim'. At home there was good country and Irish being pumped out on the radio, and that was what The Marylanders were belting out that night too. It amazed me to be up there with them, singing the songs like a true performer. All these people were on the floor and I was proud and delighted to be part of it.

The band was leading the fun and I was one of the band, at least temporarily. I relished it. What a feeling!

And the crowd was doing proper dancing – waltzes and foxtrots and Siege of Ennis. No one would just go onto the floor and shake himself, like you see in nightclubs today. They all knew how to dance back then. There were plenty of opportunities for them – ceilis, showbands, cabaret bars and the marquees.

The marquees have sadly died out. They were a great feature of our summers growing up. The local GAA or the church would put up a marquee for a fortnight, and they would get a license to hold dances there. Dances would go on four or five nights a week, sometimes every night. All the big bands would play. There might be a ceili on the Wednesday, a showband on the Friday, and a big night on Sunday. In the early days there was no dancing on Saturdays for some reason, but that changed eventually.

Some of the showbands hated the marquees. The Royal would take their holidays during the marquee season, but others were delighted to tour the tents and play to huge crowds. I remember there was a marquee in Moate, Killare, Ballycomber, and Glasson. In fact, on a fine summer's evening you could hear the music floating across the hills to our house from Glasson.

There would be great excitement in the parish. People would hang around until half ten or eleven, when the dance would start. There would be a full carnival to keep them busy until that time. There were roundabouts, swing boats, bumper cars, chairoplanes and all. There was Pongo, an earlier version of Bingo, which always drew full houses.

That would all wind down around half ten, then it was time to move over to the marquee for the rest of the night. The kids and teens would have to drift home, but the adults would spend the next few hours pounding the boards.

There was a publican in Moate called John Dolan, and he used to manage The Marylanders and arrange their gigs. Because I knew the lads, I fell in with him, and he gave me and my brother Tom work in the summer when the marquee came to Moate. We would help poster the locality before the marquee arrived, then we would help to put up the big tent, and we'd do the mineral bar at night and other odd jobs. That got me into the tent. I was never interested in dancing, but I wanted to be there. I loved hanging around the side of the stage watching the bands playing. You couldn't ask for better. I was fourteen or fifteen years old, and I was standing there selling soft drinks and soaking up the atmosphere.

That was all I cared about; getting in to hear the music. I learned a lot from watching those bands. I knew then that it was what I wanted to do, so I watched and listened intently, taking it all in. From the day I had stood up with The Marylanders and strummed John Buckley's guitar for half an hour, I knew this life was for me. Working the marquee wasn't what I wanted, but it was a stepping stone. Rehearsing with my school friends took on a new urgency – I wanted to be back on stage.

The local disco also helped foster my interest in music. It was held fortnightly in St Patrick's Hall in Moate. I went to the hops there every two weeks, where the local DJ Tom Curtin introduced us to the hits of the day. Tom did the disco on alternative weeks. On the other weeks I wasn't listening to the music. I was playing it, with Josie Adamson and Johnny Bastic, two friends from the tech. And it wasn't just the disco – we got together a number of times, for socials and fundraisers in the town and the odd pub gig. We had the confidence of youth and tore into those gigs with gusto, performing a mix of country and pop covers.

All this and I was still at school!

But I was never academically ambitious, which is just as well, because I was never gifted that way either. That said, there were some aspects of school suited me. The football was great fun, and I loved playing music with the lads in my year and ahead of me. But I had no interest in opening a book when I got home at night. Study was just not for me.

Around that time I began looking around for a job, for after the exams were over. The jobs that were prized above all others – at least in the eyes of parents – were the steady, pensionable jobs: the bank, the civil service and the public sector. In our area one of the biggest employers was Bord na Móna. They are a semi-state body that cuts turf in huge bogs along the midlands to make briquettes and to provide fuel for small power stations, among other things. Their operation in the Bog of Allen, the huge expanse of peat land that dominates the flat centre of the country, is enormous. Get a job in Bord na Móna and you were set up for life – it was safe and pensionable, and a strong union would look after your interests. Like many others I applied, and was called for an interview as a fitter. I got an offer of a position, but I never went back to take it up.

Now, to my mind, I had a good reason for turning down a great job, for I had been offered a position in Coughlan and O'Connell's hardware store, right in the centre of Moate. It was handy, being only a few miles away. I could learn the trade and have a few pounds in my pocket. But the real attraction was that they owned a pub attached to the shop. There was live music there several times a week, and I was a musician looking for gigs. Many Saturdays I got to play in the pub, in part thanks to my connection with the O'Connells.

And on top of that, one of the owners, Noel O'Connell, also managed the Roseland Ballroom, a dance hall that I haunted whenever there was a band there. If I wanted to be a musician I had to be close to the action, and I couldn't get much closer than working for the manager of the local dance hall.

So my future career – in hardware at least – was assured. In June I sat the Group Cert. To be honest, I don't even know how I got on. I never bothered to go back to the school for the results. I don't think the results would have been good – and I don't think it would have mattered. I could read, but really wasn't interested. I was better at maths. Mainly because the new master in the primary school had started us on algebra, and brought it alive. I loved algebra. To me it was a puzzle to be sorted out. But formal exams? Not for me.

It was time to move on to the next phase of my life.

CHAPTER SEVEN

WORK ALL DAY, PLAY ALL NIGHT

MICK

When I sat my Inter Cert and failed it, I drew the obvious conclusion. I had no brains – so there was no point in sitting the Leaving Cert and failing that too. At least I had brains enough to realise that! It was time to get down to the practicalities and get a job. The accordion wasn't going to pay the bills – at least not at that stage. So, just like Tony did a few years later when he left school, I apprenticed in a local hardware store.

There was a shop called James Wallace in Mullingar, and I went in there and learned my trade. I was getting in a few bob each week, and that allowed me to continue with my music. I pursued it in my own way, which wasn't the most commercial route. I didn't join a band and begin touring. I stuck to my roots. Trad was what I loved and trad was what I played. And I also loved to dance – but the two things were totally separate to me. I'd go to a ceili or a fleadh for the music, and I would just sit there listening, enraptured. And I would go to a dance with a showband if I was after the young lassies. So of course I did that too! I danced like my life depended on it.

At that time there were four women who worked in Mearescourt House. Two of them, sisters who were about five or six years older than me, were single young women full of life. They taught me how to dance. When the lady of the house was absent – which was often – we would glide through the ornate halls doing waltzes and quicksteps, Siege of Ennis, haymakers, Walls of Limerick – all the popular dances of the day. More often our impromptu sessions were confined to the kitchen. I was a quick learner and those two sisters from Ballinalea in Longford taught me well.

When the fortnightly ceili came on in the Milltown National School, I was ready. When a waltz would come on I would get up and dance with one of the sisters, and before long I was flying. After that I could ask whoever I liked to dance, because I knew what I was doing. There were lads of seventeen and eighteen – older than me – who couldn't put one foot in front of another. But I had no problems with the girls.

When I wasn't dancing I was playing. Even then I knew that you had to stand out, and the best way to stand out was to get on the radio and television, win competitions, and record. Those were the marks of the quality musician. There was the world of lads who could knock out a tune in a pub, and I had to rise above them some way if I was to make a real go of a music career. I continued to mix with trad players, learning more and more tunes. I continued to enter the competitions, and added to my junior All-Ireland by winning two senior All-Irelands on the accordion. I won the first in Clones, County Monaghan, in 1968, and then won again in Listowel in Kerry in 1970. I also managed to win six Leinster titles. Three All-Irelands and six Leinsters (between 1963 and 1970) – I wasn't doing badly.

I travelled to fleadhs all around the country. The competition was fierce, and the craic was mighty after the competitions. That was my world. *Top of the Pops* and the rock and roll on the radio passed over my head.

I think I was about seventeen when I encountered Tony Allen for the very first time. I was part of a trad group in Rathconrath who had won the All-Ireland Scoraiocht competition in 1965. One of the women in the group played the piano, and she came from outside Mount Temple, close to where Tony lived. She had a son who played in The Marylanders. I would be up in this woman's house occasionally, and Tony used to come in and out, because he played with her son. But he was just a thirteen-year-old boy, starting out, and I took no notice of him. When you're seventeen, a lad of twelve or thirteen is nothing but a curse of God nuisance. At that time, those few years represented a vast gulf.

And on top of that, he was a fierce quiet lad. But I do remember he was a great singer. He had started playing the guitar, and some of the lads locally were helping him out. Someone else started helping him on the piano.

At that stage Tony played occasionally with The Marylanders, but he wasn't yet a regular in the line-up. I was playing with Jimmy Clavin and the Black and Amber Ceili Band. The Black and Amber were a local ceili band based around Castletown Geoghegan. They soon changed their name to the Lough Ennel Band. One of the musicians was Sean Gallagher. He was the same age as me, and a block layer by trade. He played the fiddle and the banjo in the band, and we became firm friends. When I left the Black and Amber after a year or two, we remained good friends.

My next band was The Marylanders, and they were the first real band I played with. Tony was not filling in with them at that stage – he had moved on to playing with some schoolmates, and had his own gigs. Later he would join them as a full member, but that was after I left. So our paths didn't really cross for a number of years, though I knew what he was doing, and was aware of his progress. I began playing with The Marylanders in 1965, when I was seventeen years old. It was my first real band. It was different from the trad stuff. For one thing it was about keeping an audience entertained rather than the purity of the music. But it brought in a few bob, and that was the aim: to make my living at the music.

I had other things to be bothering me as well. I always had an eye for the ladies, and being a musician put me in the way of the fairer sex regularly. And I was a great dancer, which was a good opening. When I was seventeen or eighteen I met a girl who took my breath away. I still remember it well.

There was a house party in Ballymore. This man was home from America for a holiday, and the family were holding a party for him. All their friends and relatives would be there. A friend of mine, Willie Jordan, was a neighbour of the family. Willie was a good musician, and the family asked him to drop by and play a few tunes.

'And if you want to bring along a friend, feel free,' they said. Of course – the more musicians they didn't have to pay, the better!

Willie was a lot older than me. He was more my father's generation. But the music was a common interest and we went everywhere together. Who would he invite along but me? So that night I and a couple of other lads joined Willie in Ballymore, a little village between Mullingar and Athlone. We were ensconced in a corner of the kitchen, belting out the jigs and reels. I had the accordion with me, and the room was packed with people waltzing and set dancing. Those house parties could be great fun. Sadly they have died away since; that was one of the last of them, as I recall.

Halfway through the evening I looked up and saw this gorgeous young woman. She was a stunner – I was very impressed. Between tunes I asked Willie who she was. He told me that her name was Sheila Quinn, it was her uncle's house we were in, and the guest of honour at the party was her other uncle. I have never been afflicted with shyness, and

I made sure we got chatting before we left the house that night.

Things moved at their own pace after that. Before long we were going steady, then we were engaged. I was a week off being twenty, and she was a few months shy of nineteen when we walked up the aisle together and began our married life. It was November 1967, just a year after we had met. I was stone mad about her. Within a year we were blessed with our first child, a boy. Jackie was a great delight to both of us. But he was also a signal that I had responsibilities.

By then I was bringing in a few quid with The Marylanders, and I had changed my day job. I was now working with a bigger concern altogether. Chris Fitzsimons Timber Mills was a huge sawmill, and the company expanded by opening a hardware and builders' providers. I moved there from Wallace's, and I settled in. Now with a family, I had income coming in from two sources. But I also had responsibilities, and there was no question of giving up the day job. Still, I was happy.

I wasn't married a year when I saw an act on *The Late Late Show* that changed my life. They were a Scottish act, and I thought they were the best I had ever seen. I still think they are brilliant. They were the Alexander Brothers.

They had been on the go since 1958, and in fact they only recently retired after more than fifty years in the business. And from what I hear, retirement isn't suiting them! The accordion player is still mad for the road.

There were two of them. Tom was a fabulous accordion player – they don't come any better – and Jack played the piano and sang. I loved them, and they had a huge string of hits in Scotland and over here. Two things occurred to me immediately. Ireland needed its own version of the Alexander Brothers, and why was I cursed not to have a brother? I began to look around to see who might be the right man to go on the road with me.

Tony Allen was a strong candidate. He was a great singer. But, more importantly, he had a reputation for being very reliable. To find both qualities in the one man marked him out as someone to keep an eye on. I made a mental note, but got on with the business of making a living.

I wasn't long married when I left The Marylanders. I got the opportunity to play music on my own doorstep. We were living in a house under the one roof with Larry Caffrey's pub. And I was working in Fitzsimon's Builders' Providers, just two hundred yards from the house. So I could walk to work and walk home for lunch. In the evening I would walk home and have my dinner. I would clean up, then walk out my own door, walk across a bit of a yard, go in the side door of Caffrey's Lounge, and onto the stage. It was a fierce handy set-up.

I would play for two hours and put the accordion back in its case and leave it on the stage. A quick walk back across the yard and I was home. I kept that pub gig for five or six years. It was money in my pocket with no great effort, and I got to play my music regularly. There were three of us – myself, Richie Daly and Tommy Power. In addition to my accordion we had the piano, and drums. We would play traditional music, and by the end I was getting £11 a week, in addition to what my day job brought in, which was a fair tidy sum back then.

The pub gig was pure trad, which I loved. We would throw in the odd song – that was when I began singing the old come-all-yeas. My audience were there to drink and to listen to the music. They were an easy crowd. We'd often have a singer with us. We played reels and jigs and hornpipes. No one came into Larry Caffrey's pub if they weren't into that sort of music. They knew what they were getting, and it was the only pub in town providing it. All the other pubs had country music in them. So all the old fellows, and the young lads who were into the trad, came to us.

By the end I had a semi-vast repertoire of traditional music because I was learning all the time. I was learning what I wanted to play, and what the pub audience wanted to hear. At that time The Dubliners and The Wolfe Tones were big, and so were guys like Joe Dolan and Johnny McEvoy. There were so many ballads and great songs that people wanted to hear, so I learned them and other popular pieces. Every time one of these bands would bring something out, I would learn it. And I was learning new trad stuff all the time.

I still do, but not to the same extent. I've found that the older I get, the less I want to learn. Because when I learn one new tune I forget ten old ones. My brain doesn't work like it did when I was in my twenties. It's a chore to learn something new now. I have got a bit lazy – it's an age thing.

When I was young I'd play an accordion all day every day if I could. But now I don't. Just before I wrote these words, I hadn't taken the accordion out of its box for three weeks. But then, last Thursday I went to a traditional session in Roscommon – on my own, not as part of Foster and Allen. I played for about three hours, then put it back in its box. It won't come out again for another fortnight, until our next gig. That's a big change. Years ago it would never be in the case. I'd leave it lying out on a chair or on the bed, and if I had an idle moment I'd pick it up and blast into it. That's one of the changes with age.

But back when I was in my twenties I was putting in long hours at the hardware store, and still going out at night to play the music. I moved to PW Shaws in Mullingar, a concern that is still going strong. That seemed to be the pattern of my life: work hard all day and then pick up the accordion. And when I wasn't playing in the pub I was travelling all over the country, catching trad sessions and fleadhs. Something had to give. I was finding it more and more difficult to get up out of bed in the morning and show up for work.

On top of that, my family was growing. Our first daughter, Denise, arrived in 1973. There were nights of sheer exhaustion – work, then gigs, then screaming baby. But they were so worth it, to see our two children growing and developing in front of our eyes.

One of the men I travelled to fleadhs with a lot was Jack Looram. Jack was old enough to be my father, and he was as cracked on the trad as I was. We went to so many fleadhs together you'd lose count. He could see I wasn't getting any sleep and the exhaustion was telling. I knew I couldn't keep at that for ever. Jack was a small builder himself. One day he said to me: 'Can you paint a bit?'

What had I to lose? I said that I could, and he took me on for a job he had. It was a big enough job, and it took us six or eight weeks. I gave up the day job, which was a big step for a man with two children. But it suited me more. I was self-employed and if I showed up a bit late, what was the harm if I made it up at the other end of the day? But at the end of the two months the job was done, and I was at a loose end. There was no more painting.

Then Jack said to me: 'Did you ever lay blocks?'

I had never even seen a lad lay blocks! But a man can learn anything. Jack was building a garage onto a house for a fellow, and he brought me along. He led me through the basics: how to square a building, how to plumb a block and level it, and how to bob a line. Then he handed me a level and a trowel – the tools of my new trade – and said: 'Now you're an effing block layer.'

He took me through the rest of the skills I would need – how to lay the block, how to plaster and skim, and how to put down floors. And voilà – I was now a small builder, like him. I was ready to pick up work.

Sean Gallagher, another friend from the trad world, had played with me in the Black and Amber Ceili Band, and we remained close. Sean and his brothers – four or five of them – were all block layers. They went in, blocked a house, and were gone, leaving the finishing to other tradesmen. Then they would move on to the next house, while the plasterers, plumbers, electricians and roofers took over. Sean did nothing but block laying. He was a specialist. I became a good block layer myself, and I did nothing else for the next number of years, until Foster and Allen was well on the road.

I was suited enough for the block laying. The hardware store I had worked in was more a builders' providers than a shop. I had done farm work during my school holidays. So I knew quite a bit about knocking up a shed or a wall. There was very little I didn't know about the building trade. I was good at it. The only problem was that it was hard on the fingers, especially in the rain and the cold. I couldn't wear gloves, because I couldn't feel the blocks properly, and I couldn't use the level. I couldn't do the laying properly unless my hands were bare. So my hands were constantly exposed. As you can imagine, at the end of a rough day I'd have holes in the tips of my fingers. And I'd have to bring those same fingers along that evening to play the accordion. The pub gig was still going strong.

Funnily enough, after the initial experience with The Marylanders, I never played with any of the local bands. Most of the bands weren't looking for what I had to offer, and I wasn't interested in what they were doing. Brendan Shine, a talented singer who went on to become a major star, did ask me to go with his new band after he split from the Kieran Kelly band. It was a big change, but I said yes. I was all set to go on the road, playing with a travelling band. Then for some reason that I don't even know myself, I changed my mind. I decided I wouldn't go. I was living in Mullingar and he was on the far side of Athlone. Maybe that was the reason. Maybe I was fixated on a two-piece. And maybe I just didn't want to join his band. Who knows? His was the only band that ever showed an interest in me, and I turned him down.

CHAPTER EIGHT

MUSIC MAD

TONY

I followed Mick into the hardware trade – though that was more coincidence than plan!

In one sense there is little difference between your first job and your days at school. You leave home and show up early in the morning. You stay there all day, and at the end you go home. The big difference is that you get paid to show up. So now I had a little money in my pocket. But despite my newfound wealth, one thing hadn't changed: I was still music mad.

My brother Tom was as determined as ever to make it as a singer, so I suppose I had someone blazing a trail for me. The people I hung out with were musicians, and before long I began getting gigs with them.

It was through Tom that I got my start. John Dolan, the promoter who had given Tom and I work on the marquees every summer, began to get gigs for him. Tom was still working as a mechanic at that stage, and I was settling into the hardware store. It was John Dolan that suggested me for The Marylanders, and they gave me a

try-out, which quickly turned into a regular gig. It was with The
Marylanders that I began to go up front and sing the odd number,
and the more I sang, the more I liked it. The Marylanders had
grown in number since the early functions in Drumraney School,
and were now a five-piece with Mick Foster on the saxophone. But
Mick left almost as soon as I joined.

Those early gigs with The Marylanders were giving me great
experience, and were also teaching me how to work with a
bunch of other musicians. My confidence was growing.

The decade or so after I left school was probably the busiest and
most varied of my life. I went through my apprenticeship, and I
was trying to establish myself as a musician. I played in a few
different bands, gaining experience and hoping that the next one
would be the one to allow me make my living doing what I loved
doing.

The journey started in Moate, where I began serving my time
at the age of sixteen in the hardware store. Coughlan and
O'Connell was a big shop in the middle of the town. It had been
there for years, but was originally William's shop before the two
lads, Eamon Coughlan and Noel O'Connell, bought it and took
over the running of it. It was a very big concern for a place the
size of Moate, and the hardware was only a small part of it.

There was a big grocery store, the first supermarket in the
town. And they also had a bar and a lounge. During the week
days I served my time in the hardware section, and at weekends,
if I wasn't off playing with The Marylanders, I would play music
in the lounge bar with two other lads, Josie and his brother
Willie Adamson. Willie has since sadly passed on. I would strum
the guitar and sing, while they played the accordion and the
keyboard.

At the beginning I was paid £1.50 a week in the shop. That
rose to £2 after a while. But I was also getting ten bob on
Saturday night for playing in the pub. That was the equivalent

of a day's wages, give or take. I was gaining experience and getting paid for the privilege.

One evening a friend's band was playing in the pub, and my mother took me to see them. We were there for the music, as were a lot of people. It wasn't a big band – just my friend, Kevin Sheerin. He was playing with Paddy Ward as a two-piece. Kevin was a member of Kieran Kelly's band, which was a big one based in Athlone. Kieran was a talented accordion player, and he veered between ceilis and showbands. He loved the trad stuff, but he had a commercial edge. Brendan Shine was the lead singer at one stage. He went on to be a major star. One of the regulars in the band was my friend Kevin, though that night he was just doing a small local gig as a duo with Paddy.

My mother and I were enjoying the music and the craic when Kevin called out from the stage for me to sing. By that time I was sure enough of myself, so I stood and joined them. I sang 'The Shores of Amerikay', then sat back with my mother and thought nothing more about it.

But Kevin had been impressed, and he had a word with Kieran Kelly. The next thing I knew I had a job with the band. I was just sixteen, and suddenly I was travelling around the west of Ireland playing to packed halls.

When I was invited to join Kieran Kelly the money situation got even better. Kieran had a regular gig in the Irish Club in Dublin, playing a set of more traditional music. That was every Tuesday night. I'd get off a little early and we would head up for that gig, and that was worth £1.50 to me as well. So between Tuesday in Dublin and Saturday in the lounge, I was doubling my wages. That didn't happen every week, and I wasn't going to get rich. But it was obvious to me that there was money in the music business.

As much as I had loved The Marylanders, Kieran Kelly was a huge opportunity for me. The Marylanders had grown over the years from a three-piece to a far bigger concern. It had been a great starting place, because I had learned how to put dances and sets together, and I learned how to entertain an audience. But Kieran Kelly's band was a full professional outfit, touring the country. It was a big step for me, but a step I really wanted to take if I wanted to tour and develop further. This was what I wanted to do.

Kieran Kelly had a working band, and he had plenty of gigs. He wasn't as busy as some of the other bands, but that was partly because he only wanted to go out a few nights of the week. We were working in Dublin on Tuesdays, then heading west on other nights, playing in Clare, Galway and Tipperary. Brendan Shine had been in the band for a while, as the singer. He eventually left and went on to be a huge artist on his own. He travelled the world playing his music, and he still does. When Brendan left some of the band went with him. The split had happened without any rancour, but it left Kieran looking for new band members. The departure of so many musicians created an opportunity for me.

Kieran began to rebuild the band. He had already taken on Kevin Sheerin. He also hired Peter Kegarty, a fine guitar player from Athlone, and Billy Burgoyne, a drummer, and Jim Mulally, a keyboard player. And myself, of course. I could play keyboards and guitar, and sing. This was a huge step forward for me.

I think I joined in 1967, and I was with the Kieran Kelly band for about a year and a half to two years. I was still working in the hardware store by day – there wasn't enough in the music yet to give that up. I was living at home, so my expenses were not that high. They were carefree times. I had a roof over my head, money in my pocket, no responsibilities, and I was learning the music business. I was playing with the big boys now, and loving every minute of it.

The hardware store was a great fallback. It brought in a steady income, and if the music didn't take off – or if there was a bad week – I had something in my pocket anyway. I did a year in the shop, serving my time. Funnily, it was a job that got easier to do as time went on. When I entered the trade it was still a trade. You had to learn all the skills – weighing out nails, cutting glass to size, and so on. But today everything comes prepared and packed – the nails in bags, the sheets of glass in standard sizes. Now, if you can manage the till, you can do it all. I enjoyed every minute of that year. We were dealing in cement and timber and other builder's supplies as well as household hardware.

It was a big concern, the craic was good in the shop, and I had fun there. Kieran Kelly was easy to get on with, and I was enjoying my apprenticeship on the music side too. Times were good.

The Kieran Kelly band was, in fact, a huge experience for me. I was playing on a bigger stage for a bigger audience. We were bundling into cars and vans and heading off all over the country. We got a great reception whenever we headed west. Galway, Clare and Tipperary were our heartland, and we drew big crowds. We were returning home late at night, driving along empty roads after the buzz of a good gig, with money in our pockets. More and more I knew this was the life for me.

But nothing remains static. Change is the one constant in show business. Kevin Sheerin and Billy Burgoyne left to become founder members of the Hillbillies with Ray Lynam. They became very successful. Many years later, Billy and Kevin moved on again, ending up as members of Daniel O'Donnell's band. The times they were a-changing. And then I got a terrible flu. It was probably caused by leaving sweltering hot halls and jumping out into the cold night air, often into the rain. I was laid up for a few weeks, and the flu turned into a chest infection. I was barely able to move. My chest hurt, my throat was on fire, and I had a terrible cough. I couldn't travel with the band. I could barely stand. I was out of action for several weeks. To this day I have a weakness in my chest and I blame it on that time. If anything is doing the rounds I will catch it and it goes straight to my chest, dropping me like a stone. Hardly a year goes by without it hitting me again.

I eventually recovered and regained my strength, but I never went back to the band. I don't know quite why, but I could feel that it was breaking up. During my convalescence the band seemed to come to a natural end. It was time to move on, and find my next adventure.

CHAPTER NINE

LAYING DOWN TRACKS

MICK

All along, I knew that the music was the only thing that really mattered to me. And my feeling from my teenage years had not changed; it was all about getting known. I decided to record my first album. A lot of imagination and thought went into naming that LP. We called it *Traditional Irish Music with Mick Foster, All-Ireland Champion*. At least you knew what you were getting.

Naturally enough I played the accordion. I was joined by the late Richie Daly, on the piano. We went up to Trend Studios on Lad Lane, off Baggott Street in Dublin. The whole thing took three and a half hours from start to finish. It was barely more than a long gig. We sat down and played our bit, and if we made a mistake we replayed it. And if we didn't, we let it lie. It was as simple as that. Half a day in the studio and we came out with our LP, with twelve tracks on it. It was pure traditional: jigs, reels and hornpipes and nothing else.

I was just twenty-four at the time, and a few years on from winning the last of my All-Irelands. I was in serious practice, so I could just go in and sit down and belt out the tunes. I flew through it. Today I would be thumbing and fumbling. I am old enough to be exact about everything, because I realise that everything I put down now is going to be there forever. So I wouldn't want to make a balls of it. The downside of that, of course, is that you can be too conscious of what you are doing, and the playing can come across as rigid. You want the playing to sound relaxed.

Pye Records released the album for us. At that time records were priced at a golden guinea. A guinea was a pound and a shilling, but in reality the records sold for 99p. Decimalisation had come in the previous year; we had ditched the old pounds, shillings and pence, and the strange idea of 240 pennies in a pound, in favour of the decimal system. So you'd get change from your pound. It probably seemed like a bargain.

I don't know if the record ever did any business. There was no such thing as royalties. You would be so delighted to be doing a record that you would do it for nothing. Money didn't enter my head. I never saw any money from it, nor heard a word about it afterwards. I just did it because I felt it was an honour to have a record out.

The family still has a copy of it. The cover had a picture of me sitting in front of a thatched cottage near Lough Ennel in Mullingar. The thatched cottage is long gone, but that day it was crowded enough. The old couple who owned it are in the picture, and so is the piano player, and the guy who owned the pub we were playing in every night. His son was also there, and my eldest, Jackie, was sitting on a cushion at my feet. He was only four at the time. He has that album sleeve in a frame on his wall in his own house, and that is the only copy I know of.

We did a second album some time later. The cover of that one was a group in a pub, with my daughter sitting up on her mother's knee. I don't think she could even walk at the time. She has that sleeve framed in her house. The second album was called *Irish Night at Larry's*.

I was the driving force behind those records. A friend of mine, Seamus Shannon, was a good accordion player and he had brought out an album ahead of me. He explained the whole process to me. He was in with the Dolans, because he played trombone in Joe's band. And Joe's brother Ben had set up the recording for him. I knew the Dolans well, as my mentor Frank Gavigan was a cousin of theirs. So I went to them and asked them to do the same for me as they had for my friend. They were happy to oblige.

When you bring out a trad album you have no idea of how well or badly it will do. It won't hit the charts, so you can forget about the number one spot. These days, someone will buy a CD today and straight away burn off twenty copies for his friends. But in the vinyl days that didn't happen. Although I never saw any return from those two albums, they still show up regularly. I will be doing a gig in England and a lad will show up and ask me to autograph the copy he bought forty years ago.

The main point of the recordings was that they got you known. There were trad programmes on the radio, and presenters who liked that sort of music. So you would send it in to them, and it would be played. Your name was getting out there. And you had something you could give to a promoter, or a venue that was thinking of hiring you.

The rhythm of my life was now established. I worked by day in the building trade, laying blocks and trying to keep my fingers from damage. By night I joined my two companions in the pub, and we belted out the traditional music. I had two lovely children at home. Things were going well, but looking back I was probably ready for my next move. Little did I know just how life-changing that next move would prove to be.

CHAPTER TEN

PRAIRIE BOYS AND NIGHTRUNNERS

TONY

I needed to make a change. Kieran Kelly had given me a taste of what life in a good band could offer, and I was hooked. But where was my next fix going to come from? I wanted to be in a band, but where was the band that wanted me?

It wasn't easy. There was no outfit actively looking for a young lad of limited experience but great enthusiasm. If I was going to get a break, I would have to make it for myself. I looked to my friends. Aidan Grehan was a bass player from Athlone whom I had gotten to know well. When I had left The Marylanders he had joined. He was ready to try something new as well. And Tom, my brother, was at a bit of a loose end.

We got together and formed our own band. The fourth man was PJ Ward from Ferbane in Offaly. He was a good drummer. We brought in a chap from Tullamore, George Kane, to play guitar. We were ready to roll. We called ourselves the Prairie Boys and began to look for gigs. It was a good set-up. I was on the keyboards and PJ on the drums. Aidan was playing bass, while Tom was up front singing.

The Prairie Boys were more of a showband than Kieran Kelly was, and we did all right for a while. We got a few gigs. We were doing mostly relief – warm-up – work in the Roseland Ballroom, and some of the other big halls around the midlands. The Roseland was a big barn of a place in Moate. It could fit a thousand people, and on a good night often did. Now, it's worth noting that the dance halls were dry. They had a soft drinks bar, but no alcohol was served. People came for the music and the dancing. The evenings started around ten, with the relief band. The relief band was always local, and played support for the main act, which would perform from 11.30 p.m. to one.

As the relief band, our job was to warm up the audience and get them out on the floor, so that when the big showband took to the stage the place was hopping. We weren't on great money, but at that stage it wasn't about the money. It was about having a better band and improving our playing. What we were earning from the Prairie Boys was not enough to make a living. All of us had to hold on to our day jobs.

If I am honest, my finances had taken a big step backwards. With Kieran Kelly the wages were very good. I was working all week in Moate for two quid, and I was getting a pound on Tuesday and maybe the same again on a Saturday night. Some weeks there would be a carnival or a marquee, or we would travel west for a dance. Kieran was a big draw in the west. He could have been a lot busier, but unlike the other big bands, he tried to keep it to two or three nights a week.

The Prairie Boys was a step in the wrong direction in terms of money, though I guess you can't put a price on happiness and following your dreams. But on top of that, my days in the hardware store then came to an end. I left and took a succession of jobs around Athlone and Moate. I worked in a shop for a while. Then I joined Kilroy's in Tullamore as a carpet fitter. Kilroy's was a huge concern. They also sold and rented televisions, and for a while I worked in that side of the business, installing televisions and putting aerials on the roofs. Anything to keep the wolf from the door. I did a lot of things in my late teens to supplement what I could earn from the music. But my heart wasn't in any of those jobs. Music was what drew me; it was all I wanted to do.

I was only doing the various different jobs until the music began to make enough money for me to live on. I was convinced there was a living to be made out of it. As a young lad, of course, in those days a living was different to how I might understand it now. I wasn't worried about buying a house or anything, I just needed a few bob to get by. The plan was to build up to bigger things. When we were doing relief at the Roseland, we were dreaming of the day when we would be playing there as the big band. That was the plan; the various jobs were to get me by, and to keep my mother happy! I couldn't be lying in bed all day, waiting for the night and the music.

In those days, my brother Tom was serving his time as a mechanic. So he was out working every day. Neither of us drank or smoked, so that was an awful weight off our mother's mind. It didn't matter to her how late we were coming home, because we were coming home sober. I was never a great man for the drink. Now and again I might take a glass of wine with my dinner, but if I never saw a drink again it wouldn't really bother me.

Life in my late teens was all about music. I was playing as much as I could, and when I wasn't playing I was looking for gigs. Any time left over was spent at the day job. Lads I had gone to school with might have been working in Bord na Móna, the state turf and peat business, or they might have had a job in a factory. They would come home every weekend with a few bob in their pocket, and they were out on the town every Friday, Saturday and Sunday night. I wasn't. My job was to be playing on Friday, Saturday and Sunday, and if I had an evening off I would be listening to someone else playing. I wasn't really interested in the drink culture. I was never tempted. With the exception of the occasional pub, most of the venues we played in those early days were dry.

Over those rocky early years the finances sometimes were good, and sometimes dipped. With the new band the finances had taken a nosedive, but I wasn't too worried. I was living at home, and I wasn't running a car at that stage. My brother Pat had a soft spot for me and he would loan me his car occasionally. I didn't need a lot of money. It didn't take a whole lot to live in those days.

But, being in a band, transport became important. When I was nineteen and in the Prairie Boys, I bit the bullet and bought my first car. It was a cheap old banger, but it got me around. You needed some way of getting the gear to the gigs, and a car was the only option – that, or hire a man with a van to the gig and home again, which we did as well.

Though things were going well enough, us Prairie Boys knew we needed to get more out of the music. We needed a push to the next level. We got that push in the shape of Doc Carroll.

Doc was a legend in the business. Originally from Ballinrobe in County Mayo, he was one of the founders of the Royal Blues Showband, and they were huge. They were formed in 1963, and were packing halls from the beginning. They had a number one hit with 'Old Man Trouble' in 1966, which made them household names. Doc had married a local girl and was living in Athlone at the time, so we knew him slightly.

By the early seventies the entertainment scene was beginning to change. The old showbands were beginning to decline, as the cabaret lounges took over. The Royal Blues were an eight-piece, and perhaps Doc saw the writing on the wall. He decided to leave them and break out on his own.

Of course, he needed a band behind him. That is where we fitted in. We were a ready-made band, young enough for him to mould. And with what we were earning with the relief work, we were open to offers. He asked us to join him, and we said yes. The Prairie Boys became Doc Carroll's backing band.

We took on a saxophone player, John Gorman, and Doc was on lead guitar and lead vocals. We were a full showband. We changed our name to The Nightrunners and got ready to take the world by storm. Now we were a fully professional outfit. The money improved fairly quickly, and we were able to make a living from music. I was able to cut back on all the odd jobs and focus on what I loved. The Prairie Boys had given me a taste; The Nightrunners was the icing on the cake.

Looking back it was an exciting time. We were in our late teens and life seemed to be full of possibilities. The craic was mighty. We were like a team. Other lads might have been playing football or whatever. They put themselves through torture training week in week out, and for very little. But they do it for the love of the game. Our team played music. Haring up and down the country in the middle of the night when our friends were in the pub was what we put ourselves through, because we loved it. We were doing what we wanted to be doing. Doc had a Ford Transit van that had been modified. There was a second row of seats behind the cab, so we could all travel together. We would load the gear into the rear, then bundle in and head off all over the country.

With Kieran Kelly, I had been doing a lot of country-style dances and ceilis, but with Doc we were doing the showband stuff – and a good bit of rock and roll. Our audience was younger, and livelier. I loved it, and I was gaining experience all the time. I wasn't into the heavy rock myself. Country and Irish was more my thing. But I enjoyed playing it. I loved playing good dance music, feeling the beat of it, even though I never danced myself. The reaction of the crowd was enough for me.

There were long hours on the road, but we were professionals now, and we had been able to leave the day jobs behind. That was a great feeling, to be paying our way with our talent. It was as if we had stepped out of the mundane world into the extraordinarily special world of the professional musician. We would head off at three or four in the afternoon to reach some far-flung dance hall, arriving home in the small hours. But we were making a wage. In fact I was probably back to earning the equivalent of the hardware store and the few gigs from Kieran Kelly, but through my music alone. I was back up to that level. We weren't getting rich, but we were matching what a lad would have made if he had gone into a shop or a factory.

The only problem – though we didn't quite realise it – was that we had arrived at the tail end of the showband era. The sixties had been a great time for Irish music. A number of big showbands dominated the country, drawing huge crowds. The Royal Blues, the Miami, the Clipper Carlton and the Dixies were always sure of a full hall. The era spawned some big names – Dickie Rock, Brendan Shine, Butch Moore – and gave a start to a great many performers. But the music scene was changing.

One factor was the growth of cabaret venues and nightclubs. Pubs with big lounge bars would put in a smaller band and get three or four hundred people in, and all of them drinking as well as listening. The cabaret scene became highly profitable for venues, and for smaller bands willing to adjust their material to the new environment. The public voted with their feet. The dance halls were dry venues; the cabaret bars served drink. The early seventies was when it was all happening. We were ten years too late to have become superstars in the showband world.

We got a year and a half out of The Nightrunners. We were new, and that had a certain value. But eventually things began to get a bit stale. Slowly we began to go downhill. We were still getting plenty of gigs, but Doc began to want a change in direction. He wanted to go more rock and roll, while some of us wanted to go in the other direction, with more country and Irish. I can't remember what caused the final split, but one day Doc went out on his own with a rock and roll band.

The split with Doc was as civilised as you could want. We never fell out – in fact, we remained great friends up to the time of his death. He was such a lovely man, and had a great influence on my development as a musician. My time with Doc, Aidan Grehan and John Gorman is one that I look back on with great affection. All three have now sadly passed away.

We kept going as The Nightrunners, and to strengthen our line-up we brought in Mick Foster. I remembered him well from the Marylanders days. Mick began playing the saxophone for us.

I remember, from the moment Mick Foster joined The Nightrunners he was trying to persuade me to go on the road as a two-piece, taking advantage of the new cabaret scene. He wanted us to be the Irish version of the Alexander Brothers. I wasn't interested. I was enjoying The Nightrunners. It was great to be part of a big band, and that was where I saw my future.

I told Mick to give The Nightrunners six months, and it would grow on him. He told me to give it six months, and if it hadn't taken off, we would go on the road on our own. We shook. We had a deal.

I was quietly confident he would be sticking with the band.

But it wasn't to be. Fate intervened, in a number of ways. For a start we never got back to the success of our Doc Carroll days. Then Mick was involved in a car accident, and was out of action for a while. Then the gigs began to dry up. When things are not right, they are not right.

We soldiered on for a number of months. The money was still all right, but dance halls were beginning to close all over the country. Somehow, we managed a week-long tour of England. Mick was back after his accident, hobbling on crutches. Then the tour of England came to an end, and we were at a complete loose end. We had no gigs at all lined up for when we got home.

And then fate intervened again. One of the English venues we had played on our little tour was owned by a man called

Paddy Callaghan. Paddy asked Mick and I to stay around for a week and play his pub, the Prince of Wales, in Kilburn Park, North London. There was nothing to prevent us, so we said yes. We let the rest of the band leave, and we stayed for the week.

That was our first appearance as Foster and Allen, and Mick must have loved it. He was finally getting his two-piece. I wasn't so sure yet, but I had enjoyed the week, and more importantly, so had the audience. For the first time, I began to think: maybe he was on to something.

CHAPTER ELEVEN

WE'RE WITH THE BAND

MICK

Even as I busied myself with recording my solo albums and performing in the pub, the idea of the Irish Alexander Brothers was burning away in the back of my mind. And Tony Allen was still the man I had my eye on, all through that time. He had the twin qualities of talent and reliability. It is easy to find one or the other, but both together – well, there was a man worth keeping an eye on. On top of that he was a likeable man, and easy to get on with.

He had come on a lot from when I had first met him as a quiet thirteen-year-old. He was touring regularly with a number of bands, and building his skills. I knew he was the right man for the job, but it took me from 1968 to 1975 to convince him! I had to jump hoops, including spending time with his band The Nightrunners. I was touring with him and the boys, and I said to him to give up this palaver and go on the road as a duo. Our agreement was that I would stick with The Nightrunners, but if it didn't click after six months, he would come on the road with me.

With The Nightrunners I was touring a number of nights a week, seeing parts of the country I didn't know from the back of my head. And if I am honest I was enjoying the craic. I had been playing in the same pub for six or seven years, five nights a week. I was getting good money in the pub, but this was different: a new venue every night. And it was a great laugh being on the road with a bunch of young lads who all shared a common interest. Another thing I learned during those days was that I was right about Tony; he was easy to get along with.

I was messing on a saxophone. You wouldn't call me a sax player, but I would dribble into the instrument and what came out the other end was adequate. Tom Allen was dribbling into another one. We were the brass section. I played the tenor sax, and he played the baritone sax. Occasionally he'd leave off the instrument and sing a song. I sang the odd song myself, and played a few waltzes on the accordion.

We were on the road three or four nights a week, and the craic was unreal. Which is just as well, because the money wasn't great. But we were getting home fierce late in the night. I remember one night pulling into Moate and we were passing guys on bikes on their way into work. And we were just getting home from playing. At that stage I was working my own hours. I would work like a devil on the buildings midweek, then I might not show up until eleven or twelve the day after a gig. As a blockie I was paid per hundred blocks laid, so it was up to me how hard I worked. As long as the wall got built in reasonable time, I could pick and choose the hours I put in.

The days I wasn't playing I would be on the site early in the morning, and I would work like a robot, because the more blocks I laid the more I got paid. If I worked like hell I had money in my pocket at the end of the week, and if I didn't work, I had nothing. It's a bit like now: if we tour for a month we make money, but if we sit at home we earn nothing. So things haven't changed that much, but the music is easier on the body than the block-laying!

I suppose for a while I was burning the candle at both ends. Though I wasn't drinking I did enjoy the attention of the fans. Maybe I had a bit of a roving eye.

There was a great camaraderie on the road, and savage craic in the van. If we were playing the west or the south-west we would stop in Limerick on the way home for a bite to eat. There was a cafe on Nicholas Street, in the shadow of King John's Castle, called the Treaty Cafe. We called it Dirty Dick's. We'd always stop there around midnight or maybe even later, depending on where we were coming from. It was a sit-down take-away. You could get chicken and chips, or maybe a greasy fry. The waiter, Eamonn, was a music fan and he had the world of vinyl LPs. And every band used to stop there, not just us. By three or half three in the morning it could be packed with maybe five or six different bands, all talking loudly and swapping stories. We got to know some of them fairly well. It was one of the great joys of the road.

I don't know how it would all have ended if fate hadn't intervened. The Nightrunners was a bit of a success. We got gigs, and audiences liked us, but it was not going as well as it could. Perhaps we could have built on it. But we didn't get the chance. I had an accident.

I remember it well. We were doing a gig down in Cork somewhere. I can't remember the exact venue – there are so many of them that they become a blur after all these years. But I do remember travelling home that night. We were travelling in a van and a car. The van was being driven by Tony, and two of the lads were with him. All the gear was in the back. His brother Tom was driving the car, a Fiat 127, and I was sitting beside him in the passenger seat. Two of the lads were behind us.

We came to Mallow, a big town about twenty miles north of Cork city. It was around midnight, and we were less than an hour from Dirty Dick's in Limerick. We were wide awake and chatting. Tom may have been a bit heavy on the pedal, and we were travelling fast. Suddenly we came to a T-junction. I don't know how he missed it, but he did. He hit the brakes far too late.

I couldn't leave well enough alone. Like an automatic pilot, I braked too, even though I was in the passenger seat. I threw my leg forward and pressed my foot into the well in front of the seat. The tyres squelched on the road and we skidded across the junction, still moving far too fast. There was a low wall on the far side of the road, and we slammed straight into that. What the brakes couldn't do, the wall did: it brought us to a sudden stop. My foot was still extended out straight in front of me, and as we struck the wall I heard a sickening crack above the bang of the collision, and pain shot through my leg.

We juddered to a standstill, and Tom looked around. He was uninjured. The two lads in the back were, like James Bond's martini, shaken but not stirred. No one was injured, except me. My leg was broken in two places. It was shattered. And I had no one to blame but myself. If I had kept my legs under me where they belonged there wouldn't have been a problem.

The break was every bit as bad as I feared, and I was out of action for the next seven months. I had plaster up to my thigh for much of that time, and hobbled around on crutches. There was no question of being able to stand for two hours and hold a saxophone. I was off the road. I was also out of work – a one-legged blockie is not very welcome on a building site. It was a dole job. I had to sign on and bide my time while nature took its course and the leg healed. My young family and I were under horrid pressure.

Meanwhile, the band soldiered on, but the decline had set in. Gigs began to dry up.

Eventually I was ready to return. I still had a bit of a plaster, and the leg needed building up. But I was on the mend. The Nightrunners got a week in London, and I set my heart on being ready for that. The London tour was the recovery target, and I did recover in time. We went out and did a week of gigs there, and they went well. I enjoyed them. At that time there was a decent circuit for bands like us in England. There were about ten venues in London, and they were good venues – cabaret and concert halls rather than just Irish clubs. Like in Ireland, though, things were changing. The venues were no longer dance venues; it was now cabaret they wanted.

One of our gigs that week was at the Prince of Wales near Kilburn Park tube station. It was a big bar owned by an Irish man, Paddy Callaghan. The Nightrunners went down well there, and after the gig we were sitting down chatting to Paddy. He asked us what we were doing the following week, and we had to admit that we weren't doing much. We hadn't a single gig lined up. We were feeling the pinch.

'Why don't you stay on here for a week, and do a few days in the Prince of Wales?' he asked. It was not a general invitation; he just wanted Tony and me. We were at a loose end – what did we have to lose by staying back? I would play the accordion and Tony was on the keyboards and taking most of the singing duty.

Foster and Allen was born.

Another Irish man living in London was Pat Nolan, and he gave us a lovely little PA system for the week. (He has since moved home and has a big band-hire business in the midlands.) Luckily, it wasn't difficult for the pair of us to prepare for our first two-piece show – we were used to pub gigs. I was more used to them than Tony, but he was a quick learner. He knew most of what I was into, and I knew what he was into, so we had no difficulty putting together a programme for those first few shows.

For that first week in London we called ourselves Mick Foster and Tony Allen, which was a bit of a mouthful. We played a full week in the one venue. It was just like any normal pub gig back home – but it felt right, straight from the start. This was what I loved, and what I had dreamed of since 1968. So you could say, of course it was going to feel right to me, whether it was right or not.

But I knew from the audience reaction that we were on to a winner.

They loved the music. Tony did a bigger share of the singing; I provided the fast jigs and reels. The mix of trad, ballads, and folk and country just seemed to work.

Ireland finally had its Alexander Brothers.

CHAPTER TWELVE

LIBERTINES AND LIBERATION

TONY

So, The Nightrunners went to London, but Foster and Allen came home!

We had seen how well the duo had gone down in that one week in London, and looking back now, I don't know why we didn't commit to that format straight away and go all out for it. However, nothing in life is ever as simple as it should be. We tend to overcomplicate things. Perhaps it was a lack of confidence. Or perhaps we thought that if two was good, two with backing would be better. Maybe something of the big-band era still clung to us. Whatever the reason, when we came home, we put together a four-piece instead of a two-piece as our next band, but we aimed it firmly at the cabaret circuit. We were leaving the showbands behind us.

I suppose Mick would have looked at us as the Alexander Brothers and Friends, instead of the Alexander Brothers. We called ourselves Liberation. It was an RTÉ sports commentator, Jimmy Magee, who gave us that name. Jimmy is a household name now, in the twilight of a wonderful career. He is known as the Memory Man, and he has forgotten more about sports than most of us will ever know. But he has far more talents and interests than that. In his early years, while he was following boxers, golfers and hurlers around the country, he was also heavily involved in the music business. Jimmy worked with Release records at the time, in addition to his RTÉ work.

When we came home from London we got two lads on board – Sean McCormack and Vincent Kenna. Mick was a great believer in recording albums as a way of standing out from the crowd. It was also a great calling card at new venues. If they liked the LP they might take a chance on us. So we went into the studio and recorded an album of traditional tunes and ballads. We all put in a few quid to fund it, and hire the studio for a few days.

I was a novice when it came to recording. It was my first time in a studio. Mick knew exactly what he was doing, since he had a few traditional albums out already. But I found the whole experience a bit daunting, until I got used to it. We were rehearsing a good deal, and playing regularly together, so it wasn't that difficult in the end. But that first afternoon in the studio was a huge experience for me. When you are playing for a live audience there is a huge energy. But in a studio there is nothing. You have to build up your own enthusiasm or the playing will suffer. However there is another way of looking at it: without the pressure of an audience you can try out different things. If it doesn't work, you just do a second take.

That first album took just two days to record. We went into the studio, the engineer gave us the nod, and we sat down and did our thing. It was so tightly rehearsed beforehand that we could work quickly in the studio. And apart from the odd second take, I was fairly happy with my first foray into the world of recording.

Two days after entering the studio, Liberation's debut album was ready to be pressed onto vinyl.

Then we began to look around for someone to distribute it. We met with Jimmy Magee, and with Mick O'Riordan, who was one of the heads of Release Records as well as being heavily involved in the Irish Music Rights Organisation. Both Mick and Jimmy loved the album, and they agreed to bring it out for us.

But Mick O'Riordan knew it was as much about marketing as it was about the music.

'It doesn't matter how good you are. You have to be different,' he told us. 'Look at you – what is the difference between yourselves and any other band out there?'

We looked at each other and shrugged.

'What should we do?' we asked.

'You need to dress differently,' he answered.

At the time *Barry Lyndon* was the big movie hit of the year. It starred Ryan O'Neal, and was about an eighteenth-century Irish adventurer and chancer. It took four Oscars, and everyone in the country went to see it.

'You need to dress like the man out of *Barry Lyndon*,' Jimmy Magee suggested. As we had already taken his advice on the name, it was an easy step to take his advice on the costumes.

When it came to shooting the photo for the sleeve of the album, we followed Jimmy's advice. We went to a dressmaker and described what we wanted, and she got some curtain material and made them for us. They were based on what a gentleman in eighteenth-century Ireland might have worn on a good night out. We had leather brogues with buckles on them, topped with white knee-length socks. Then we wore breeches that came down to the knees, frilly shirts with lots of lace on the collar, and jackets that came down to our thighs. We were colourful and distinctive. I cannot remember now who wore what, but we had a black, a yellow, a brown and a red coat. No one was going to mistake us for the stage crew in those costumes!

Looking back the outfits might appear a bit peculiar, but at the time we took them for the most natural thing in the world. We wore them for all our gigs over the next number of months. We were playing regularly in pubs and the big cabaret lounges, and they made us stand out from the other guys doing the same circuit. I was on guitar at that time, rather than keyboards, and Mick was playing the accordion. One of the other lads played the bodhran, and another the uilleann pipes, the Irish version of the bagpipes. We gigged around the country as much as we could, and we even brought Liberation to London, touring the Irish circuit there. But the album had not done well, and our set-up was a bit limited for the cabaret scene. With the pipes and bodhran we were leaning heavily towards the traditional. We did sing the odd song, but our material and our approach just weren't commercial enough. And the suits weren't enough to make the difference. Just like The Nightrunners before, we saw our hard-won gains dwindling away. We could get work, but not enough to keep four of us on the road. I could see failure looming.

By the autumn of 1975 the writing was on the wall. Vincent and Sean were finding it increasingly difficult to juggle their day jobs with the band. They felt they had to leave. Vincent, the bodhran player, was the first to go. He was involved in the building trade, and he couldn't afford to walk away from the good money for the meagre pickings Liberation offered. Then Sean left, so we were without bodhran and pipes. We found it hard enough to find replacements willing to come on tour with us. It is a strange thing, but trad players do not seem to relish life on the road as much as other musicians! We soldiered on. We were still getting the gigs. But it was becoming more and more difficult to keep it together.

Finally we let the two new lads go, and we decided – at last – to try our luck as a two-piece. Foster and Allen had worked in London. Might it not work in the cabaret lounges of the Emerald Isle?

It was a case of being in the right place at the right time. We had missed the showband era by a few years, but the cabaret scene was booming in the seventies. Makem and Clancy were huge, as were The Wolfe Tones, Misty, and the Dublin City Ramblers. The big acts tended to hit the big venues on a Thursday or a Friday night. On a Saturday night the patrons often wanted to dance. This suited us fine; our music could be dancing music as easily as listening music. For the remainder of 1975 and on into 1976 we concentrated on growing our business as a duo, and getting as much exposure and as many gigs as we could.

We had a two-pronged approach – marketing, and the old stand-by of producing an album. Mick wanted that – he pushed for us to go right back into the studio and hammer out an album as Foster and Allen. That first album was recorded in Castleblaney, County Monaghan. The studio was owned by Big Tom, the lead singer with the Mainliners. He was one of the huge stars of the showband era, and a major name in the music business. Billy Burgoyne, who had worked with me before as part of Kieran Kelly's band, was our producer. He got in a number of session musicians to fill out the sound, with Mick and myself up front on the accordion and keyboards. We called the album *Mick Foster and Tony Allen – Traditional Irish Cabaret*. A bit of a mouthful, but it got us some airplay on the radio, and that is what it was all about.

I still remember the sleeve. It was a brown cover, with just Mick and me on the front, surrounded by a load of instruments. By that stage we had got new suits. They were made by Jas Fagan. He dressed the whole music business. The suits were green, but this time they were cut from proper suit fabric – there would be no more curtain material for us. We used to bring that LP around with us, and sell copies after our gigs.

It was also our calling card with new venues.

One of the first things we did as Foster and Allen was to drive up to Dublin and spend an hour in Eason's, the big bookseller on O'Connell Street. They carry all the provincial papers there, and we bought up every one they had – *Limerick Leader*, *Sligo Champion*, *Kerryman*, *Munster Express*. We walked out of the shop looking like paperboys about to start our day.

When we got home that evening we spread the papers on the floor and opened each one to the entertainment pages. Back then there could be two or three pages of entertainment ads. There were so many pubs and cabaret venues that had music regularly. There were probably 75 to 80 per cent more than there are today. We followed a simple marketing strategy: we would pick a county – say Cork – and look through the two or three pages and identify any venues that had a group similar to us playing. Any place that looked suitable, we wrote them a letter explaining who we were.

Mick was a three times All-Ireland champion.

I could sing.

And we had been around a bit.

Those were our credentials. And, of course, we had the album. And once they got the letters and the album, very few venues failed to contact us and offer us something.

Phones were a rarity back then, so most business was done by letter. But my brother Tom was married by then, and he had a phone in his house. His wife Therese very kindly acted as our unpaid secretary for a time, in between minding her baby sons, Don and Gary.

It didn't take long before our engagement book began to fill up. Within a couple of weeks we had a full schedule, and Foster and Allen was no longer a dream in Mick's head.

It was a reality.

CHAPTER THIRTEEN

JUST THE TWO OF US

MICK

Where Liberation had failed, Foster and Allen worked from the beginning. I had always had reservations about having more than two in the band, because I was still tunnel-visioned as regards the Alexander Brothers. To me they were the business – no one else compared. There were some great Scottish acts on the go, but they could have been painting pavements for all I cared. And the Alexander Brothers were packing places in Ireland so I knew I was right. And so it has proved!

Our first gig on Irish soil as Foster and Allen – more than six months after our debut in London – went very well. Though we weren't quite Foster and Allen yet – we were still Mick Foster and Tony Allen. There were about fifty or sixty people in the pub, Dowlings of Prosperous in County Kildare, and they all enjoyed the evening. We played all Irish material – ballads, rebel songs, and whatever was on the go at the time. We tore into everything. Rebel songs were very popular, and some bands like The Wolfe Tones specialised in these. They were seen as Republican bands. We avoided that tag by singing the older rebel songs. We rarely sang modern ones, and tried to keep our material non-political. We preferred the old songs – more Dubliners than Wolfe Tones.

Tony sang the occasional country song as well, because these were very popular. But we didn't stray too far from my roots. Every third number was Irish music. Pure trad – I loved it.

It was a simple set-up. Tony was behind the keyboards and doing most of the singing; I was standing there with my accordion, and taking the odd song – the ones that weren't too difficult to sing! There is no doubt we were good at what we were doing, but I think a key part of our success was that we were the only ones doing it. We had no competition. Our line up was significantly different from everyone else's, and so we thrived. We still have no competition, because no one is offering exactly what we offer. I knew there was a niche there, and we filled it on our own. Our success wasn't because we were better than the rest, it was because we were different.

And the costumes helped. Within a short time we got new costumes made, and this time we got them made in green. Green breeches and green jackets. Audiences loved the green suits, and we got very comfortable in them. And, further down the line, when we appeared on television we wore the suits as well. The look was as important as the sound if you wanted to be a commercial success.

And the seeds of that success were sown right from that very first gig in Dowling's of Prosperous. Dowling's was a very well-known cabaret lounge where all the ballad groups played, so it had good form as a starting venue. Christy Moore recorded his second album there in 1972, and called it *Prosperous*.

We got the gig easily: we sent an LP and a letter to the manager, and he wrote back and gave us a date. We performed for the princely fee of £30. But more important than the fee was the fact that we were invited back there. We returned a number of times over the next few years, always to an enthusiastic crowd.

Pubs were going well at the time, and we drew a good crowd that first night. They weren't there for us, but that wasn't important at that stage. What was important was that they enjoyed our music – and they did. A good crowd is a relative term, and in some of those venues fifty or sixty people was good. A year or two later we were putting 800 into pubs, but that was when we became better known. We used to play in Greenacres in Carlow, a ceili and old-time venue. There was a cover charge of 50p, and if you didn't do 500 people, they didn't want you back. If an act starting out drew 500 today, he would be going around with a swelled head. It would be very hard to talk to a fellow for three or four days after that. But there was no chance of Tony getting a swelled head. That was one of the reasons he was the right man for the job.

It was always Tony I had in mind for the project. He is a very easy man to work with. Both of us would be wasps – we don't suffer fools gladly. I would fight with my own fingernails, so I am probably a bigger wasp than he is. But despite that we haven't had an argument from the sixties to today. Not over anything. So something about us works.

Tony is a great singer and a good piano player, and that was what I was looking for. I wanted someone who was reliable and good. And they are hard to find in the Irish music scene. Either they are real good and unreliable, or they are not worth a shite but they'd never let you down. The bottle is a terrible curse – so many talented musicians are drinkers, and you can't depend on a drinker. I knew a number of guys who were very reliable. If you said you were leaving at eight, they would be there at ten to eight. If you said you were going to Botswana, they'd have their bag packed before you got off the phone. But you might as well leave the hoors in Botswana, because they were no good.

Tony combined the qualities of reliability and talent. He was the man. It helped that he was a good singer. I can sing a bit, but I wouldn't be a good singer. I camouflage my singing by sticking to comic songs and come-all-yeas. But Tony has great quality to his voice. He can sing anything, and that is important.

We are good friends, and in forty years there has never been a hard word or an argument between us. But we don't live in each other's pockets. We rarely socialise together, or go out to dinner together, unless we are on tour. For one thing, we live hours apart. Both of us love horses, and we might meet up at a race meeting somewhere. But it would be by chance. Tony is stone mad on GAA, but it's football he loves, and I prefer hurling, so we wouldn't meet at a game. I'm into handball, and I don't think he has ever seen a handball game. Our interests don't coincide, so we rarely meet outside of touring, recording and playing. But since touring, recording and playing take up half of our year, we see a hell of a lot of each other.

But make no mistake: we get along famously. There has never been a bad word between us. We have an unwritten rule. It is so unwritten we have never even talked about it, but we are both aware that it is there, and has been from day one. If the two of us don't agree about something, we don't do it. If Tony said he thought we should tour Yugoslavia, and I said I had no interest, it would never be mentioned again. Or if I suggested a new outfit for the stage, and he said it wouldn't suit us at our age that would never be mentioned again. Unless both of us agree completely, it is gone. It is not just shelved, it disappears as if it had never even been brought up.

In a lot of bands there is jealousy and petty rivalry. One man might want to sing a song that another guy wants, or one man might feel he should be more to the front. It leads to friction. We seem to have escaped all of that. We never clash over songs because the bottom line for me is that I don't want to sing at all if I can get out of it. I am an accordion player and nothing else. And the stuff I do sing, Tony wouldn't have any interest in singing anyway. The stuff he sings, I wouldn't be able to do. There are no egos in Foster and Allen. We leave those to the young lads.

Years ago, when the showbands were still on the go and we had just started, you'd be invited regularly to perform at local concerts or Lourdes fundraising shows, and similar events. For most of the showband performers it was important who went on last. If you went on last then you were the headline act, at least in your own mind. Everyone else was playing support for you. So they used to fight bitterly over that last spot. But we used to fight over the first spot. Get the first spot and you got home early.

There was a great country duo called Two's Company who were performing at that time, and they'd cottoned on to this idea too. They were Eamonn McRory and Mary Darcy from Carlow, and we met them regularly on that circuit. There was no clash in material: they were pure country, while we were Irish, trad and a bit of Scottish. But there was a clash when it came to performing position. We battled it out to see who could get on early and go home. The problem was that no promoter would follow a duo with another duo, so if you missed that early spot you were stuck there until the second half. We'd argue the toss, but the solution was simple: whoever was ready first went on first. And the loser sucked it up, and was stuck there until after the interval.

Oh, it was comical to see the hullabaloo to get ready. I'd be hopping around trying to get into my costume, and Mary Darcy would be running around half in and half out of her costume, trying to beat me. Sometimes she won; sometimes I did.

Right from the start there was no ego in Foster and Allen. We were old enough not to be sticking out our chests and saying we were the greatest thing since sliced bread. At those concerts it never bothered us who was on before us or after us. We went out and did our own thing. If people thought we were good that was great. If they thought we were useless we didn't get too bothered. We took the business seriously, but we never made the mistake of taking ourselves seriously. How can you get a swelled head in Ireland about singing or playing the accordion? Singers and musicians are ten a penny. There's always a lad around the corner who's better than you will ever be, but you do the best you can. If the public think you are good, then you are good. It doesn't matter whether you are good, bad or indifferent, it is the public's judgement that counts in the end. They'll tell you where you stand, and if you can't accept that, it's your loss.

The biggest adjustment for me was learning how to connect with an audience. When I was a brat playing traditional accordion I just went out on the stage and played. All the people cared about was listening to the tunes. It didn't matter if I had snot hanging out of my nose or the arse hanging out of my trousers as long as I was playing well. So, as often as not, I was looking at the floor. But that wasn't good enough for a duo on the cabaret circuit. This was the commercial world, and it was important to look at the crowd and smile a bit. You had to engage and involve the audience. That was a knack it took me years to master!

Thankfully I was always good at the banter between songs, and that helps me make a connection. And Tony, though he is not as good at the banter, can really get a crowd going when he plays. It's a powerful feeling looking down from the stage and seeing an audience loving what we do. You simply can't buy that feeling.

And with Foster and Allen pleasing the crowds at seemingly every gig we went to, it was a feeling that – against all odds – seemed set to last.

CHAPTER FOURTEEN

LIFE ON THE ROAD

TONY

For the first year and a half to two years we managed ourselves, and we did a good job of it. There was no week that we didn't work.

But that said, and as great as that was, we could see there was still room for improvement. Bands like us – and there were a lot of them around – were worth forty quid a night. Yet that was well short of the big time. A band like Misty would have been worth £150, and The Wolfe Tones were making astronomical money, because they were a big draw. They would fill any hall in Ireland. Looking at the competition, Foster and Allen still had a way to go.

But £40 a night wasn't bad. You would come home with £20 or £30 after petrol and other expenses – including the chips in Dirty Dick's in Limerick! It easily exceeded the average industrial wage of the time, but not enough to make us rich.

But we were doing well enough. We would work a minimum of three nights a week, and often five nights. There were plenty of cabaret venues in the country, and it was rare that we played a place and weren't asked back. Slowly, we were building up both a fan base and a regular schedule that kept us happily in employment, living our dreams as working musicians – although at the very beginning we were still working the day jobs too. But those regular bookings were never to be sniffed at. We worked hard as anything to keep the gigs rolling in and the repeat bookings repeating, time and time again.

Mostly it was just Mick and me on the road, but after a while, occasionally a friend would join us, and act as our unofficial roadie, and he would also sell the records after the gigs. Tommy Cushen and his wife Mary were friends of ours who lived in Moate. Tommy was in the army, and based in the barracks in Athlone. On evenings he would be off duty, he would come along with us for the ride. It was great to have an extra man for the gear. He was a great help for us, and good company on the road. During the late seventies and early eighties he was with us often.

Things were going well for us, and we began to collect material for our second album. We didn't know how it would do, but we knew we wanted to put it out there at least. It would be called *The Blacksmith*, and we began laying down tracks. Instead of doing the whole thing in a mad dash over two days, we would record a track when we had one ready to record, and when we had a few hours to visit the studio. I was getting more used to the recording process, and found it fascinating.

We also shot the front cover picture. We had a picture taken of the pair of us at an old Irish forge.

Slowly but steadily, we were beginning to inch our way toward success. We were making a good living, and our tracks were beginning to appear on the radio.

All we had to do was hang in there.

CHAPTER FIFTEEN

OUR FIRST BIG BREAK

MICK

From the beginning, everything about the two-man set-up seemed to work. By 1977 we were busy enough for me to give up my day job. I no longer had to get up bleary-eyed and try to lay out a layer of blocks. Tony had already given up the carpet fitting and the hardware work. We were professional musicians at last.

We had a cheap van on the road, thanks to the help of my father Jack. It was an old banger of a Volkswagen that had seen far better days by the time we got our hands on it. We bought it in 1976. It had been a bread van and had been in a bad crash. A garage in Kildare had it, and my father had dealt with that garage, Fitzpatrick's, for years. He bought all his cars there. We negotiated a price of £700, and he loaned me the money. The sliding door had been badly damaged in the crash, and it was still strained. It whistled as we drove, letting in the cold air. But the engine was sound and it didn't let us down.

Due to the strain on the door we would often be driving along with the cold wind whistling in our ears, and it wasn't a pleasant tune. The natural air-conditioning was leading to running noses and stiff backs! Often we would try to seal the gap with bundles of newspaper, but it rarely worked as well as we hoped. Another problem was that the heater only worked properly if we could build up a bit of speed. I will never forget driving home from Donegal to Mullingar, almost a hundred and fifty miles, on a damp and dreary St Stephen's Night. There was dense fog and we were stuck in third gear, chugging along at a snail's pace for most of the journey. The slower we went the worse the heater functioned, so we were like two frozen penguins when we arrived home.

On foggy nights or in the rain, when the roads were slippery, we suffered the chills.

On another night we were coming home from Limerick, and we had to get out in Birr and run up and down the street for a few minutes, trying to pump some life back into our frozen limbs. Happy days. We persisted with that van for two years, until we were in a position to buy a new one.

I was still living in Rathconrath, and Tony was in Mount Temple, about twenty miles apart. We would meet up and hit the road. Apart from the occasional, very unofficial roadie, we would lug our own gear and set it up at the venues. But that was no hardship; there was feck all gear. We had three microphones, a keyboard, an accordion, two speakers, an amp, and an echo unit for the singing. It was a simple set-up. We switched on the amp and turned it up. If it squealed, we turned it down again until it stopped squealing.

I still remember it all – even the brands. The amplifier was a 200-watt Dynacord, and the speakers were Crazyboxes, which were big enough and gave great sound. It was a Benson echo.

We had gone through every cursed of God newspaper in the country looking for venues, and we had sent out hundreds of letters and LPs. That got us gigs the length and breadth of the country – from Wexford to Monaghan, from Galway to Louth.

I think we covered the entire twenty-six counties. Most of the places we contacted gave us a try. Once we got in, it was up to us to do a good job to ensure that we got back in the following year. And in the vast majority of the cases, we did.

There was the odd place where something went wrong – maybe there was a poor crowd on the night, or they felt we played too much trad. Or too little. But in general we got back everywhere, so we were building up a solid circuit of work. But it's funny how it is the off nights that stand out, not the good.

I think it was in 1975, but it might have been the following year, we played a gig in Limerick city on Christmas Eve, in a venue called The Brazen Head. It was right in the heart of the city, and no one showed up. There were about a dozen people in the bar. That was our worst crowd – or if not our worst, at least our smallest. But the twelve that were there that night were brilliant. They gathered around us and we had an almighty sing-song. It was a lot more informal than most of our gigs, but it was a wonderful night. Wonderful – but after that we didn't give up another Christmas Eve with our families to face an empty hall.

In contrast, we did one night in Taylor's of Shillelagh in Wicklow, and the place was jammed. They were swinging off the rafters, there were that many inside. If someone turned to the bar to order a drink, everyone had to turn, they were that closely packed. And they loved us that night. But what I've never understood to this day was, we were never asked back to that venue. I could understand if we stank the place out, but we hadn't. I still wonder about that night.

In 1977 we got our first big break, with a television appearance. I had done plenty of broadcasting as a teenager and young man, on the trad shows, and I knew how much exposure you got from those few minutes on the flickering screen. Television would give us a great boost, but it would not be easy to swing that. There was tremendous competition for the few prime slots.

Our break came through Joe Mooney from Drumshambo in County Leitrim. Joe used to run a festival, An Tostal, in the village every year. We played for him a couple of times, and got to know him. In addition to promoting the festival he was involved in politics, serving as a member of Seanad Eireann (the second house of our Parliament) and Leitrim County Council for Fianna Fáil. We also knew his son Paschal, who was the same age as me. Paschal was into the music, and presented music shows on RTÉ. Eventually he followed his father into politics. He is currently a senator.

We were chatting with Joe in 1977, and I said to him that a slot on the television would do wonders for us.

'Are you trying to get on?' he asked.

'We're doing our best,' I replied.

I told him about all the broadcasting I had done as a teen, and he told me that he was great friends with Liam Ó Murchú. Ó Murchú had been more than a decade with RTÉ at that stage, as editor of Irish language programmes. He had his own television show, *Trom agus Éadrom*. This Gaelic phrase means heavy and light, and that described the show to a tee. He would interview some of the political heavyweights about the issues of the day, then maybe talk to a musician or a hurler or a local dog show organiser. The show was a mix of the weighty and the trivial, and was conducted half in English and half in Irish, and was very popular.

'I'll give Liam a call if you like,' said Joe.

Promises are as ephemeral as ice cubes in a bowl of boiling water, but he was as good as his word. A few weeks later we got a call telling us that we would be on *Trom agus Éadrom* when the show came to Athlone next. A few weeks later the cameras arrived, and we were there waiting for them, in our best green suits. I remember we did a slow song about a rebel being held in the jail at Clonmel – the Jail of Cloonmala. Liam must have liked us, because it was the first of many appearances on *Trom agus Éadrom*.

The next day, every lad was talking about our appearance, just like in my school days. We had only one television channel, so there was no escaping us. For months we got it everywhere – 'I saw you on *Trom agus Éadrom*', 'Do the song you sang on the telly'. Every hoor seemed to have heard us, which I was delighted about. You couldn't get that exposure today. I have about a hundred channels at home, and 95 of them are not worth a curse. And what you'd want to see you'd miss because there are so many options.

I don't think that first television appearance made much difference when it came to getting gigs, because our diary was full anyway. We were not expensive, which was a good selling point! And it didn't make much of a difference to our fees, but it certainly increased our crowds. That is why it was so important to us. People who had seen us on television came out to see us live when they saw the ads in the paper or the posters outside a pub.

We appeared on *Trom agus Éadrom* a number of times, and on a few other programmes too as our profile grew. But those early television slots exposed a flaw in my performance. We were a few years into Foster and Allen, and doing well, when we appeared on *Donncha's Travelling Roadshow*, a summer variety and chat show presented by Donncha O'Dulaing. That evening it was coming from Adare Manor, a luxury hotel in the picturesque village of Adare, just south of Limerick city. We were doing Irish music, with me on the accordion as usual and Tony singing. We were barrelling away in the rehearsal, and I was delighted with the way things were going. But I was alone in that.

The producer was going wild. He told the floor manager to get the hoor with the accordion to smile. The floor manager was diplomatic; he said that things were going well, but could I smile a bit more. I tried to oblige. But the problem was that every time I smiled I made a mistake. My concentration went from the instrument to the imaginary audience, and I missed a note. It was a disaster. In the end I had to say to him: 'You can either have me smile and make a bollocks of it, or do it right and let me do it my own way.'

'You'd better do it right, I suppose,' he said. But I could hear the reluctance in his voice.

Another problem was my accordion style. I was a big Jimmy Shand fan from the days of twisting my granny's gramophone with my fingers as a five-year-old. I had seen Jimmy play since, and he wouldn't open his accordion more than the width of his palm. All he needed was enough air going through the reeds to produce a noise. He didn't need the exercise of clapping his hands in and out while he was playing. I had learnt at the feet of Frank Gavigan, who wouldn't open out the instrument more than the bare minimum, so that was my style; it barely moved in my hands. I was what was known as a lazy accordion player.

But a lazy accordion player is damn all use to a television camera. They want action. I heard it all the time from producers and floor managers: 'Would you not pull it out and push it back in a bit? You look like you are miming.'

They might as well have asked me to fly to the moon in the van going home as ask me to pull out the accordion more than I needed to. I wasn't able. Smiling, and being animated with the accordion, those were the things at the commercial end of the business that I found difficult to get accustomed to. I smile now, but I still don't pull the accordion in and out. And I talk to the audience more instead of looking at my shoes. So I am making progress!

With the airplay from our records and the bit of television exposure, we began to stand out. The Dubliners, Barleycorn, The Fureys and The Wolfe Tones were still at the top of the pile, and we weren't threatening them. But of the average middle-of-the-road, not-too-expensive acts we were the only ones with a record out, and with the odd television appearance behind us. That made a difference. We rose a bit above the others.

And we played and played – there was no life outside of the touring. But, year by year, things were improving for us. I remember playing a gig in our early days in the Refinery Club in Cork. The gig was promoted by a local taxi driver, Liam Foley. It was a three-hour ceili, and we were paid £80. He supplied a drummer to fill out the sound, and an MC, so we weren't rushed off our feet between the numbers. The next time we were back there we managed to beat the price up to £100. Soon after that – when we were with CMR Records, and were getting regular airplay – we were £150 a night. That wasn't bad money, especially if you were doing five or six or even seven nights a week. It was a lot more than our day jobs would have paid.

But it wasn't all plain sailing. There were still spots where we struggled. The bane of our life was south Limerick, and a band called the Boys in Blue. They were from the village of Athea, and they drew serious crowds all over south Limerick and north Kerry. If you were anywhere in that neck of the woods and you drew a bad crowd, you could bet your shirt on it that the Boys in Blue were on the road. They were a persecution – they cleaned us out. To this day I don't know whether they were good, bad or indifferent. All I know is that every time we came up against them we lost. Other bands, like Johnny Barrett, you could take your chances with, but we learned to avoid the Boys in Blue whenever possible.

Bingo was the other great curse. It was our main opposition. If you were in Newcastle West, County Limerick, and the bingo was on there as well, you might as well stay at home. Our audience was older people, and they loved the bingo.

Most of the time we tried to get our forty pounds from the venue – and as the years went on we tried to push that forty up a bit. But sometimes we had to do a deal on the door. Working on the door is quite common in the entertainment industry. You charge an admission to the gig, and pocket whatever comes in. Sometimes the venue will want a percentage of the door, but more often they will be satisfied with the bar takings. If you fill a venue, they will do well. It is great for the venues – they have no risk. But for a performer it is not so good. You had to be wary of doors, because a pub that was going well would not give you the door. The owner would know he was going to make money. If a lad offered you the door you knew it was because no one was coming to his pub. Unless we were sure we would draw a crowd, we would say no: 'The roof of the van is bent carrying doors. Give us our fee.' That was the holey all of it.

But sometimes we took the chance, and sometimes it worked out spectacularly in our favour. This became truer as we became better known.

However one of our greatest successes on the door came right at the start of our career. In early 1976, just a few months after we began and before we had packed in the day jobs for good, we approached a pub a few miles away from us. It was about three or four miles out the road from where I had grown up in Moyvore, and the owner had built on a lounge to the side of the bar as a singing lounge. He would have local groups in regularly.

I knew the man well from living down the road all my life, so I asked him if there would be any chance of a night in his bar. He told me he'd be delighted to put us on some night. This was good news – gigs close to home are always welcome. Then we started to talk money, and things quickly went south.

'What sort of money would you want?' he asked.

'Forty pounds,' I said. It was our usual fee, and just because he was close to home there was no reason to come down. We were well worth it.

He didn't think so. He spluttered. Forty pounds for a band was unheard of, he told me.

'I'll give you twenty,' he said. 'There's a man up the road who is a great musician, and he wouldn't get forty. I only give him twenty-five. I couldn't give a new act like yours a penny more than twenty pounds.'

The man up the road might or might not have been a great musician, but he wouldn't draw his breath outside of the locality. Arguing wasn't going to get me anywhere, but I tried my best.

'We play down the road in Abbeyshrule and we get forty pounds. How would it look if we played here for twenty? We'll have to leave it so.'

I got up to go, but as I was heading out he called after me: 'You wouldn't be interested in taking the door at fifty pence?'

If it hadn't been so close to us I probably would have walked away, but I decided to take a chance. We shook on it, and had our deal. On the night the place was stuffed, and we ended up taking £150 on the door. It was a great haul for us back then – the bones of a week's gigging. And we would have been willing to have played for him for £40. If he had been a little less cautious that profit could have been his. We played that venue a few more times over the next year or two, and we pushed the ticket price up to a pound, which pushed our take to £300. On the very first night he lost a potential £110 for himself because he wouldn't go the extra £15 and meet our regular fee.

We did well in odd places. Kennedys of Pucane was one of those. Pucane is a tiny village in Tipperary on the shores of Lough Derg. It is a beautiful place, very popular with tourists who come up the lake on cruisers and stop off there for the night. We were on the door there one night, and due to go on at nine. By a quarter to nine they had to bolt the door, there were that many people inside already. The man doing the door for us had a thousand pounds in his pocket before we took to the stage. After expenses there was still the guts of £500 for me, and £500 for Tony. That was huge money back then. Our fee would have been far less than that.

It really was astonishing to see how our career took flight. The money was one thing, but it was the enthusiasm of the crowds that took your breath clean away. Those first two or three years as Foster and Allen were tremendously exciting. The audience got what we were doing, and our crowds steadily built. It was nothing spectacular, but from 1975 onwards we made steady, solid progress. It was not an overnight success; it would take a full ten years or more to reach our full potential. It was a slow, steady build – but you could argue that is the best kind of all. Foster and Allen had found a niche, and we were filling it well.

For the first time in our lives, we were on the road to success.

CHAPTER SIXTEEN

'THE RAMBLES OF SPRING'

TONY

We were building things nicely on our own, but then we got a real break. Getting management makes a big difference to any band. There are two great advantages. The first is that someone else is doing all the legwork, making the calls, sending out the letters and albums, and handling the paperwork. So that leaves you free to concentrate on the music. And let's face it, none of us got into the business to do paperwork! The second advantage of professional management is that they are probably better at it than you would be yourself. People tend to play to their strengths.

We were lucky enough to get Donie Cassidy on board towards the end of 1977, after nearly three years of handling ourselves. Donie was steeped in the music business. That's where he differed from Mick and me. We were steeped in the music, and could handle the business. But Donie was a businessman who happened to work in the music industry.

He was a couple of years older than us, and in fairness he was a musician first. So he knew that side of the business very well.

He was from Castlepollard, in the north of Westmeath, so we knew a lot of the same people. Donie was a talented man on the saxophone, and he was part of the line-up with Jim Tobin and the Firehouse. They were a showband with a heavy country slant and they got a top five single in the charts ('This Is It', 1970). Donie was managing them – in fact, at that stage he wanted to move fully into management. He was looking to find someone who could take his place on the saxophone in the band.

As well as artist management, he had his own record label, CMR Records. The record company and artist management became the backbone of his success. Around that time he also had a television project on the go. *Opportunity Knocks* was a talent show in the UK, which was one of the top-rating programmes every week. It was presented by the late Hughie Green. Donie set up an Irish version of the show. The semi-finals and the final were televised on the new national television station, RTÉ2, and he hired Hughie to host them.

Donie eventually became a senator, for Fianna Fáil. But that was a long way in the distance. A friend of ours, Toss Martin, suggested that Donie should check us out. He knew Donie was on the lookout for musicians for his own band, as well as acts to manage. He planted the seed: he told Donie that we could do well if we were handled right.

Donie came and heard us play, and he must have liked what he heard. After the gig he said: 'Drop over to the house and we'll have a chat.'

We met up and drove up to Castlepollard one afternoon. It was obvious from the start what he was after; he wanted Mick to play the sax and the accordion in the Firehouse. But we were firm: we weren't interested in any new bands. We were doing good business on our own, and that was what we wanted to continue with. When he could see he wasn't going to get his way, he changed tack. He said he would manage us.

Tony: Here I am at 3 years of age with my parents, Patrick and Rose.

Tony: Me at 17 years of age.

Mick: On my First Holy Communion day with my parents Jack and Jane Foster (*left*) and grandparents Tom and Mary Foster.

Mick: Me aged 21 after winning Westmeath, Leinster and All-Ireland Senior Accordion Trophies, 1968.

Tony: Me with my family. There were nine of us in total. *Back row, left to right*: Jack, Pat, Margaret, Mick (RIP), Beasie, me, Tom. *Front row*: Anne, my parents Patrick and Rose (RIP), and my sister Mary (RIP).

LEFT: *Tony*: With Doc Carroll & The Nightrunners, 1973. *Back, standing*: John O' Gorman (RIP). *Middle row, left to right*: Tom Allen, P.J.Ward, Aiden Grehan (RIP). *Front row, left to right*: George Kane, Doc Carroll (RIP), and me.

RIGHT: Foster & Allen begins! With our first van, circa 1978.

LEFT: In our style suits in the early years.

BELOW: With BBC Radio and TV presenter Gloria Hunniford.

LEFT: With former World Featherweight Boxing Champion Barry McGuigan.

Mick: With Sheila and the kids. Our twins Sandra (*right*) and Louise (*left*) are in front and Denise and Jackie are at the back.

ABOVE: On tour with our Canadian tour promoter, Leo Puddister. It was a double sell-out.

LEFT: A career highlight performing at Croke Park, Dublin during the 1988 Cork v Meath All-Ireland Football Final. Donie Cassidy stands between us.

At our Gold Record Presentation at Warner Music, Australia in 1997 with Ken Harding (*back row, right*) and Margaret Harding (*front row, left*).

At the recording of our 21st anniversary special on *The Gay Byrne Radio Show* at RTE. *Left to right*: Mick, Joe Dolan, Tony, Daniel O'Donnell and Charlie Landsborough. DAVE CULLEN PHOTOGRAPHY

Here we are with Champion Jockey A.P. McCoy at Cheltenham, 2003. Both of us have a great love of the races. HEALY RACING PHOTOGRAPHERS

On location, filming one of our videos. It was always great craic.

HUGH GLYNN PHOTOGRAPHY

Mick: A proud grandfather with my grandson Daniel taking his first ride at a point-to-point in Durrow Co. Offaly, with trainer Cecil Ross and Carol Ross.
HEALY RACING PHOTOGRAPHERS

Mick: With my first accordion teacher, Sister Agnes, who taught me as a student at Ballymahon Convent of Mercy.

Mick: With Tony and my two grandchildren, Sarah and Daniel, and Tom Gilmore of the *Tuam Herald*.

Tony: On my wedding day to Trionagh. *Left to right*: my sons Ian and Keith, Trionagh, Ian's wife Su and Trionagh's sons Lee and John.

Tony: My son Ian with his wife Sutanya and my granddaughters Ava and Surin-Rose.

Filming our Sky TV show, December 2012. *Left to right*: Peter Cassidy, Mick, Terry Wogan, Michael Bracken and Tony.

JOHN O' CONNOR
PHOTOGRAPHY

With the band. *Left to right*: Seamus Cullinane, Tony, Moyra Fraser, Ollie Kennedy, Mick, Brian Megahey.

Foster & Allen: Still going strong, after all these years

BARRY MCCALL

That was the start of the turn for Foster and Allen. We were two or three years on the road by that stage, and managing ourselves. We weren't doing badly, but he was able to build us up from that initial base we'd established for ourselves. Our first record as Foster and Allen had come out under EMI. But Donie's record company took over for our second album, *The Blacksmith*, which we were already working on. He began to help us find tunes, and advised us on what would sell and what wouldn't. He was able to get the music into the shops too. We were no longer just selling them at the backs of halls.

The first thing he was able to do was get us plenty of airplay. Back then sponsored programmes were all the rage. Every afternoon on the radio there were a number of quarter-hour and half-hour sponsored programmes. They were a mix of music and chat. Many of the record labels and music promoters sponsored programmes as a way of promoting their acts. Donie Cassidy Promotions was one of the companies that had a show. Some of the others were Tom Costello Organisation, Noel Carty Promotions and Release Records.

With all his contacts Donie was able to get us plenty of airplay. With a little bit of planning and cajoling he could make sure our record got played every day, and maybe a couple of times a day. With no competition to RTÉ Radio, that meant that the whole country heard you. If they liked what they heard, they would come out to see you. Donie was also able to advertise our upcoming gigs, which was a great help.

'The Rambles of Spring' was our first song to do well. We brought it out as a single some time after hooking up with Donie, and it became very popular. It was a fast tune from Tommy Makem with a good lively chorus that people could sing along to.

'The Rambles of Spring' didn't chart, but it got huge radio play, and it got our name out there. We were out every night of the week, and we were playing full venues. The attention from that record brought us to the next level.

Now we needed to find an equally strong song to follow it up. We knew only too well: you are only as good as your last success.

CHAPTER SEVENTEEN

SUCCESS ... AND SADNESS

MICK

With Donie as a manager, we hoped that he would build upon the success that we had created for ourselves during the first few years of Foster and Allen, gigging around the country. In fact, Donie was getting us airplay, but live shows were still the main event. Of course, we didn't have the luxury of a roadie to drive us around the country. We had to do that ourselves. As I remember it I did most of the driving – but Tony might remember it differently! I certainly started off each journey, and drove us to our venue. We would share the drive on the way home, when tiredness was creeping up on us.

The old banger of a Volkswagen got us through the first two or three years on the road. Despite its draughts and its noises, it got us where we were going. But the time came when we wanted a bit of luxury – and we were beginning to make the money to afford it. So in 1978 – around the time we began to be managed by Donie Cassidy – we decided to bite the bullet and buy a new van. It was a sign of our confidence in the duo –

we had been busy for two or three years, and there was no prospect of it slackening, so we felt we could take the chance.

The problem was, we had no credit rating. We were musicians, with no guarantee where our next few bob was coming from. If you went into a bank and explained what you did for a living they would point to the door and say try closing it from the outside. Getting a loan or a hire purchase was out of the question.

If we had gone for a loan two years earlier, when we were making far less money but were working a trade, it would have been easier. At that stage we still had day jobs, and we would have got a sympathetic hearing. But there is always a way. One of my jobs, before I had started block-laying, was with a builders' providers in Mullingar, Fitzsimons. I knew the proprietor Chris Fitzsimons well. I had worked for him, and had wound up manager before I gave the whole thing up. Chris had diversified and had other interests besides the builders' providers and sawmills. One of those interests was a hire purchase company called Leinster Finance. He was worth an approach.

I went in one day and asked him to give me a loan of £10,000. He knew what we were at. But he also knew us – he knew we were working hard and doing reasonably well. He gave us the loan, and a year to pay it back. The interest rate was relatively high, but beggars can't be choosers, and we took the deal.

We bought a brand-new Hiace van. And like the first car my family owned – the Baby Ford – I still remember the registration number: 1099 LI. We were working a fierce lot at the time, and we had the money paid back to him within the year with no difficulty. Then it was time to upgrade our equipment. So I went back to Chris, and explained that we needed to invest in the duo. He gave us another £10,000 at the same rate. We were able to buy some great gear, and again we paid it back in time.

That was when we got the Rolls-Royce of speakers, Crazybox. They were about three feet high and threw out a great sound.

We got a good amplifier, good microphones, and spare mikes and leads so that we could never be caught short. It was the best of equipment and it brought us through the next few years. We could produce savage sound – there was no venue we couldn't fill.

With new wheels under us, and good equipment in the back of the van, we were happy to set out for all corners of the country. I kept the van at my place, and I would drive out to meet Tony. If we were going north or east he would come up to my house and we would go on together. If we were going south or west I would pick him up at his house. And if we were going north-west we would meet somewhere like Ballymahon. He would park his car there and hop into the van.

Back then the pubs were open until eleven in the winter, and we played nine to eleven. In summer, closing time was eleven thirty, while on Sundays it was always ten o'clock closing. We played the final two hours of the night. We would start right on the button of nine, even if there was no one in the venue. On the button of eleven we would strike out the National Anthem. Our show was over. The odd lad would crib that we couldn't start until the venue had filled up a bit. But we never budged. And the next time we would be back there, they would troop in on time. We educated them to suit ourselves.

If we were beginning at nine, we would make sure to be there by eight at the latest. We didn't linger – within fifteen or twenty minutes we would have all the gear in and the leads in place ready for a quick sound check. The sound check was basic – if it wasn't screeching and they could hear us at the back, we were done. The equipment was good, so we knew the quality of the sound was right once we had the levels right. Then we had plenty of time to change into our costumes and be ready for a punctual start.

Tony was still playing the piano and organ at the time. That was the way it went, from our start in 1975, through the years

of turning professional, the early chart success, and on to the
end of 1982, when we were successful enough to take things in
a slightly different direction by bringing on two extra musicians.

In our first few years we would definitely have been out five or
maybe six nights a week. Sometimes we were out every night.
Come the late seventies, in July and August we would do seven
shows a week, week in week out. There were no days off during
the summer months. It was non-stop. We were probably making
more money back then than we are doing now, we were gigging
so regularly. The gigs were plentiful and we only had to split the
fees between the two of us. We were working like hell, but we
were young and we had the energy and drive for it. Doing a two-
hour gig was nothing to us. In fairness, it is still easy on us. We
enjoy it as much as ever.

If you enjoy the music, it doesn't feel like work up there on
the stage, and time seems to fly. As I write this I can remember
last Sunday week, when I met up with a few friends of mine
from Birmingham and Leeds. They are traditional musicians,
and they were over here in Ireland on holiday. We went into a
pub and played together for four hours, just for the fun. No one
was paid – we did it for the pure love of the music, just to please
ourselves. And the four hours felt like a few minutes.

Just last Saturday, too, I played at a traditional concert in
Cavan. I only did fifteen minutes in the concert, but afterwards
ten or twelve of us played in the bar for three hours, just for the
craic. If that is how I get my fun, you can imagine how two
hours on a stage was a doddle, and still is.

After every gig, we made an effort to get home. When you
have a young family you want to be back with them in the
evening. As I had driven to the gig, Tony would drive
home, or at least halfway. I might take over if he got tired. The
only exception was when we had a linked date. If you were
doing Cork tonight and Killarney tomorrow night, it made
sense to stay out. But if it wasn't a linked date, we always went

straight home. We couldn't afford not to. And it could be very late by the time we would finally pull in. I often passed lads going to work when I was just getting in from mine. They thought I was mad – but I thought they were mad. We were in total agreement with one another. We were all mad.

Tony and I might be great company for each other in the van, or we might not. We could get into the van and talk for Ireland for the first fifteen or twenty minutes, then there mightn't be another word spoken until we reached Limerick. One of us might fall asleep. One of us might put on the radio.

We were lucky that we had loads of friends and relations scattered around the country. There weren't many places we didn't know someone. My mother came from Moneygall, and if we were heading towards Limerick my aunt Moll was still in the village, and always had a welcome for us. She is in her nineties now, and livelier than I am. We could always call in to her for a good meal. Or there was a lass from Moate who worked in the Two Mile Inn in Limerick. Mary Martin would often be home in Moate and we would give her a lift back to the hotel. So if we were coming home from Ennis and passing through Limerick we could drive into the hotel and she would bring us in and give us a mighty feed.

She is living now in Aberdeen. She and her partner Robert run the Aberdeen Douglas Hotel, and we stay there whenever we are touring that neck of the woods.

I have already mentioned the Treaty Cafe in Limerick as a fierce haunt for bands and groups. It was serious craic. And there were similar spots in other parts of the country. We got to know them all.

Life on the road was uncomplicated when there were just the two of us. We made all the decisions on what we would play together. We never had an issue on that front. What Tony would be singing I couldn't do, and half of what I was singing he wouldn't want to. It is the same to this very day. We have different abilities and different styles, and we pick what suits ourselves, and there is never a clash. We are so close in one way, and so far away in another way, that there would never be a danger of us clashing over material. We just sit down together and he will say what he was going to do. I would say what I was going to do. Then we would see how the two knitted together. Sometimes that would mean Tony would have to change something, and other times it would mean I had to change something. We might have to add a number to bring up the time, or drop a number to bring the show back inside the two hours. But it was as simple as that – never a hard word spoken.

We have always chosen what we would play in a concert or cabaret show. And for years we chose what we would record as well. But with success comes complications. Now our record company has a say in that side of things. In fact, they have the major say. For the past ten or fifteen years, our recordings have been influenced by London. They want what they know people will buy.

Of course, we do have some input. But once it is commercially driven, they have a huge input too. In the early days it was a lot more free-wheeling. Those early days were a pure joy to me. Both of us were in a bit of a rut when Foster and Allen began. We were playing for bands that were going nowhere fast, and labouring at the day jobs to make ends meet. To be on the road was like letting out a young horse. He would be cooped up in the stable all winter, and then you would let him out into the fresh air and he would buck and roll and run, and be delighted with himself. It was the same for us. Those early years were absolute magic.

And when we started touring abroad, it was twice as good.

The only downside for me was that I had a wife and small kids waiting for me at home, and I missed them fiercely. That was awfully hard – it was dreadful. This was in the days before mobile phones. If you were away from Ireland for a month, you had to send post cards.

But I always felt that no matter what you do, there is a price to pay. If a man has success in one aspect of his life, he will lose out somewhere else. The way life catches me might not be the way life catches everyone, but it will not all run smooth all the time. That's true on the road. But it would be equally true if I had stayed at home building walls and sheds, or sweeping the roads for the council.

I believe that for every success in life, you have to pay for it. Though on balance I believe I have been blessed with a great life, for every success there must be a payment. That is my personal belief.

And sadly, just as our success as a duo started to build, I experienced a family loss that set me reeling. My mother – despite her many health challenges – lived to see the start of our success. She passed away in June 1978, at the age of fifty-eight. She lived long enough to see Foster and Allen on the road and our first television appearance together. But my mother did not survive to see that success blossom. I was devastated when she died. It is a terrible setback to lose your mother. We were expecting it on one level, because she had been ill for so many years, but that does not take the sting from it. It was still a tremendous shock when it came.

Thankfully my father had many more good years ahead of him.

And, I hoped, so did the band.

CHAPTER EIGHTEEN

'A BUNCH OF THYME'

TONY

By 1977, everything was going well for Foster and Allen. We had a brand-new red van, with our names emblazoned in white on the sides, no less. We had great new gear – the best that was available at the time. And we now had management. Everything was in place for success.

But just as Mick says, for every silver lining, there has to be a cloud. And in my personal life, too, tragedy struck.

Just as we were beginning to get our first taste of success, deep sadness touched both our lives. Mick's mother and my mother died within a few months of each other. Mick's mother had been ill for years, but nothing prepares you for the sense of loss. I sympathised deeply with him.

My own dear mother Rose passed away in September after nearly a year of sickness. She was only 63, and even though she had been battling cancer and we knew in our hearts that the prognosis was not good, we didn't really think we would lose her. Having said that, not one of us would have wanted her to suffer for one more single day. It is something we never really got over.

Over the next few years, as our success grew, I wondered if those two ladies were pulling a few strings up in heaven for us. Maybe they were teaching the angels our tunes...

They were certainly looking out for us when 'The Rambles of Spring' was released. That had got enough airplay to get people interested in us. Now we needed a follow-up to build on that success.

As it turned out, I was the one who found the song that pushed us to the next level. It was a song first recorded by Christy Moore, a rising young folk singer, and I loved it from the moment I heard it. I just needed to get others to believe in it the same way. I started with Donie Cassidy. At the time we were putting together our next album, and we had agreed on twelve songs. We were looking for two more.

I remember the evening well. It was in the winter of 1978, and it was bitterly cold outside. Donie and his wife Anne were down in my house chatting. They got up to go, and when I opened the front door a blast of winter came barrelling in. It was beginning to snow. Ireland does not have the best weather in the world, but one thing you can depend upon is that the snow won't last. I suggested they come back inside to let it pass, and I would put on the kettle while we waited.

We sat down with our mugs of tea, and to kill the time I put on some music. I had a box of LPs under the couch, and I pulled them out. One was by Christy Moore, and it had the song I loved on it, 'A Bunch of Thyme'. It was a traditional folk song, and I think it came from the north of England. That is certainly where Christy picked it up, while he was touring there. On the surface it is a gentle love song, but it carries a hidden message: beware of giving away your love too freely. It is that hidden edge that lifts it out of the ordinary and makes it such a great song.

Mick and I had played it at several of our concerts. It was a quiet number, and I noticed that when we played it the dance floor cleared, and people would often chat during it. But those were pub gigs; they loved the waltzes and quicksteps, but the slower ones did not get the same reaction. I still thought it was a great song.

Donie and Anne listened to it that night, and they both enjoyed it. They agreed it would make a good album track, so it went on our list, as song number thirteen. We had agreed to record it.

When we went into the studio to finish recording *The Blacksmith*, we also recorded 'A Bunch of Thyme'. The sound engineer on that album was Philip Begley. Liam Hurley, brother of the singer Red Hurley, was the producer. He knew his music and he loved the new song. I could see it in his face – afterwards he was raving about it. He was another convert.

In fact, he loved it so much that he phoned Donie that evening, and told him we had a potential single. This was far stronger than an album track, and we shouldn't throw it away. Donie agreed to release it as a single towards the end of 1979.

And, oh boy, was Liam Hurley right. 'A Bunch of Thyme' got played off the air! People loved it, and it climbed rapidly through the charts. Some presenters took a great shine to it, including Val Joyce, who had a very popular Saturday afternoon show, mixing sports and music. The whole country listened to *Airs and Races*, and they could not avoid our new song. Val Joyce played it until he had the vinyl worn out. 'A Bunch of Thyme' entered the charts on 28 October 1979, and within a few weeks it had climbed all the way to number one.

Those were exciting weeks – every Sunday we would anxiously wait for the charts to see where we were, and when we hit the top spot, we were jubilant. It was unbelievable. And the song wasn't done yet. It remained in the charts for forty weeks, then re-entered two years later for another three months.

This was the culmination of years of hard work. All the late nights, the countless gigs, the paperwork, and even all the hours of practice as young lads starting out on this journey. Nothing would be the same again now. The whole country knew our music. We were the best-selling artist in Ireland for a number of weeks. Oh, they were heady days.

If 'Rambles of Spring' had made us known, 'A Bunch of Thyme' made us household names. Suddenly everyone knew who we were, and when we got to venues the crowds were waiting for us.

Our future looked secure.

CHAPTER NINETEEN

A HOOR OF A SPIN

MICK

We were finally doing well, after years of struggling, laying bricks until my fingers were numb then grinding out jigs and reels in a pub, or touring the country with bands that were going nowhere.

But life proceeds at a pace that takes no prisoners, and we couldn't rest on our laurels. It was soon time to make our next move. And it was a big one. Deciding to tour America was a huge step for us, because it was a hoor of a spin out there. But in 1981 we were invited out to the States to tour, and it would be impolite to say no to this great opportunity.

Actually the truth is that like any young band we loved being given the opportunity. We were more than delighted to make the long journey, and to play our beloved music well beyond our country's borders.

I don't recall the exact circumstances of the invitation, but I know it came through Tom O'Donoghue. Tom had a big pub and restaurant in Pittsburgh. Pittsburgh is an industrial city in Pennsylvania. It is about the size of Cork and has a thriving Irish community. Someone must have put us on to Tom, or Tom on to us, because it was through him that we went out.

Back then you couldn't fly into Pittsburgh. Aer Lingus offered the choice of New York, Boston, or staying at home. We flew into New York. Tom had organised the entire tour for us. All we had to do was get to the venues and do the shows. Most of the venues were Irish centres and Irish bars, and we were playing to the American Irish. There was a strong market for that back then, and many bands went over. It was a great experience, but there were so many of us beating that trail that you would not get rich on it.

We landed, and we had a van waiting for us. It was hired for the two weeks of our mini-tour. The gear was hired as well – though I brought my own accordion, of course. When we arrived in New York we were able to ignore the big queue of people clearing immigration – we had done that in Shannon on the way over. So it was straight out to the car park to locate our van.

It was a very successful tour, and we got a great reception everywhere we went. The Irish-Americans are a friendly race, and they loved to see us play. We played intimate venues and we were treated like old friends. That's a funny thing about being abroad; a lad that would run away from you at home would be all over you when you got to America or Australia. That's because you're a link with home. You talk the same way as their parents do, or the people they remember and miss. So they will come and hear you. It is the same to this very day.

America was our first real tour abroad – because the UK was only a boat ride away, and almost felt like home. We were nobodies in America; just two Irish lads playing their music in the Irish bars. In that way it was like our early days touring at home, before we got the airplay. It was a return to our cabaret roots.

But the distances involved could be savage. Tom had set up the tour, hitting all the Irish communities along the eastern seaboard. We visited cities such as Boston, New York, Pittsburgh (where he had a great welcome for us), Philadelphia and Washington, as well as more isolated Irish centres in Maine, Connecticut and Massachusetts. We headed as far west as Chicago, which is right in the centre of the country. But that is as far as we got that first tour – or on any subsequent tour, for that matter. There are vibrant Irish communities further west, and down south, but we have not toured there. Yet...

The roads were great, but it was tiring all the same. We were driving on the wrong side of the road and in strange places with no familiar landmarks. So there was no relaxing.

The first tour was a great success, and a wonderful experience. About the only downside was being so far away from home and the kids. My family had grown again – in 1980 our twins, Sandra and Louise, were born. I could phone home, but that meant tossing an endless stream of dimes into a pay phone and hoping someone was there at the other end. And, of course, I couldn't speak properly to the children, or see them grow and change. Still, it was just two weeks for the US tour that first time out, and it had to be done – it was my full-time job, after all.

When we were asked back again a few months later, we were delighted to return.

Our second tour of America was in March 1982. I remember that trip chiefly for two things. The first was that the logistics of the tour were less well thought out than the previous year. We had a gig in Boston one evening, and the following evening we were in Philadelphia. They were the two furthest extremes of our tour, and only a promoter, sitting on his arse in an office, would think of linking those two locations! We had a ten-hour drive to get to Philadelphia. Then we had to do the gig, with very little time to catch our breath beforehand. I get tired even thinking about it now.

The second thing that stands out is how the tour finished. We ended in New York City, a great place. We were scheduled to have a day or two to relax and see the sights. We could buy some souvenirs for home. We were looking forward to seeing our families again, as always, but there was also another reason we were looking forward to going home this time around. We knew 'A Bunch of Thyme' was back in the Irish charts – but it was also making inroads on the charts in the UK. That was exciting – only a few Irish acts were lucky enough to chart across the pond.

We had been getting updates from home about the progress of the song, and our sense of excitement was mounting. And then, as the tour ended and we prepared to relax for a day, we got a call from Donie telling us to drop everything and get to the airport as soon as we could. We had to fly home immediately. 'A Bunch of Thyme' was climbing so high in the UK charts that we might be on *Top of the Pops*.

I had never seen *Top of the Pops*. I had barely even heard of it. I wouldn't watch it in a million years. But I knew it would be a great break, in that it would get us savage publicity.

Foster and Allen had hit the big time.

CHAPTER TWENTY

THE LEPRECHAUN INVASION

TONY

Our trip to America was cut short – and we were over the moon as to why. But to explain how we were on the verge of appearing on the iconic show of *Top of the Pops*, we need to go back a little bit.

'A Bunch of Thyme' had been good to us. Reaching number one in Ireland in 1979 got us plenty of airplay. Irish television was a great help – we appeared on *The Late Late Show* and *SBB ina Shui*, as well as programmes presented by Donncha O'Dualaing, BiBi Baskin and Liam Ó Murchú.

All those wonderful programmes invited us to share our music, so we went from being just another cabaret act to being a well-known name in the business. When we pulled up at a pub and began lugging in our gear, the people knew who we were. Venues were clamouring to book us.

If we had still been managing ourselves that would have been the full story: more gigs, more recognition, and a full diary.

But now Donie Cassidy was looking after us, and he was in the record business as much as he was in the live music business.

He thought that the success of 'A Bunch of Thyme' in Ireland could be replicated in the UK. He went over to London and did a deal with a record company.

He had high hopes.

Many Irish artists were doing well at the time. Joe Dolan had had a number of hits, and had matured into a mainstream pop act. The Dubliners had had a hit with 'Seven Drunken Nights', which got them onto *Top of the Pops*. The Fureys had charted with 'When You Were Sweet Sixteen', a slow ballad that had reached number one in the Irish charts, so he saw an opportunity.

Unfortunately it was not as easy as that.

His initial efforts saw the song sink without a trace. I thought that was the end of it, and didn't give it another thought. Meanwhile Mick and I were getting ready to tour America for the second time.

We had toured America for the first time in 1981, and had enjoyed the experience. We did well over there. The older people loved us, but it was an exclusively Irish and ex-pat audience we were playing to. The communities we played were full of Irish people, and there was a great buzz everywhere. They loved the Irish acts, so many acts made the trip. The Chieftains, The Dubliners, Paddy Reilly, Makem and Clancy, all those acts were huge. So were The Wolfe Tones and Barleycorn, with the more rebel ballads. Hal Roach, Noel V. Ginity and some other comedians also played the circuit there.

It was great craic but you couldn't build a career on it as there were so many others doing the same thing. Our second American tour was in March 1982, coinciding with the excitement of St Patrick's Day.

But – almost unbeknown to us – forces were working away at home. A man called Mick Clerkin had set up Ritz Records in the UK in the early eighties, and he had a few hits with Irish acts. It was he who had helped The Fureys reach number sixteen in the UK with their song 'Sweet Sixteen', and which had broken the top ten in Australia. Mick Clerkin was pushing them for a follow-up, but they had nothing ready.

Mick had an Irish office close to Westland Studios, where we had recorded 'A Bunch of Thyme'. Donie's office was close by, and Donie was never a man to pass up a chance. He called on Mick and persuaded him to release our song on Ritz Records.

So as we were jetting off for America, our song was beginning its assault on the British charts.

It did very well. Our single broke into the top forty. Things were looking good. Mick Clerkin rang Donie and told him the good news.

The song had some great champions. At the time Terry Wogan and Gloria Hunniford were two of the biggest names on the BBC, both with their own popular radio shows. And both were from Ireland. So 'A Bunch of Thyme' got plenty of plays over the weeks of February and March, while we were in America and oblivious to its progress.

Then, on 15 March, Donie got another call.

'Where are the boys?' asked Mick. 'We might need them for *Top of the Pops*.'

'They're touring America,' Donie told him.

But Donie knew that the tour was almost over.

Top of the Pops was a huge break, if we got it. It was the most watched music programme in the UK, and it was also shown on RTÉ every week. It was massive; it made careers. It was a countdown of the top charting singles every week, and anyone with any interest in music watched it religiously. I know that Mick wasn't interested, given his love of trad music, but I watched it myself whenever I got the chance. I remembered seeing many of the Irish acts that had been on it in the past.

Top of the Pops was a lot more than a music programme; it was an institution. As a teenager, I would watch it every Thursday night without fail, and the following day at school we would all discuss who had been on, and which acts we had liked. It shaped the musical tastes of a generation, and sparked more schoolyard discussions, rows and impromptu air-guitar sessions than any other show.

In the sixties I had seen The Dubliners on the show. They were an incongruous act, a complete contrast to what else was on. Joe Dolan had a few hits in the UK – 'Make Me An Island' had hit number three – and of course I had seen him perform.

One memory I have of the programme is of watching Tony Christie with his song 'I Did What I Did For Maria', on a new television at home. Just Tom and I were watching, and the following day it was all the talk in the tech in Moate.

I think everyone in the country except Mick Foster tuned in at some stage! Mick had very specific tastes in music, and *Top of the Pops* is a bit light on jigs and reels for him. But even he appreciated the enormity of the opportunity it would be for us.

We had just finished our tour of America when the news filtered through that we might get the call. We had a few days off to explore New York, and spend some of the money we had earned on the tour. We were due to fly home on Thursday. But Donie told us to get out to the airport and come home immediately. That was on Monday.

That night we caught the Aer Lingus flight home. We touched down briefly in Shannon, then flew the final thirty minutes to Dublin, landing on Tuesday morning. At the airport we picked up our bags and bundled into a taxi, which took us to Lombard Street, where Donie was waiting for us.

It was tense. Mick and I were exhausted. We sat in the office with Donie. I don't remember much chat. I think that Connie

Lee, who was entertainment manager at CMR Records, was also there. But despite our exhaustion we were very excited.

Even Mick was.

At twelve o'clock the phone on Donie's desk rang, and he snatched it up.

From his grin we knew the news.

We were going to London.

Foster and Allen would be on *Top of the Pops*.

It was an unbelievable moment. A year previously I had watched The Fureys with Sweet Sixteen. Little did I think then that I would be following them on the show a year later.

We were delighted, but we didn't break open the champagne. Mick and I were never great drinkers, and Donie didn't touch a drop. But he did send out to O'Dwyer's pub, on the same street as the office, for a round of drinks. I can't remember now what we had, but we did toast the news in true Irish fashion. It was great, but it was so strange for us. We thought that we would go on the show, and that would be it.

Little did we know it was going to be the start of a huge career.

After our impromptu celebration we relaxed for a few hours, then Mick and I caught the last flight to London. It all happened so quickly. We stayed that Tuesday night in the Mulroy Hotel in Kilburn. It was a great hangout for the Irish bands. We had stayed there often, when we were doing gigs in London. It was a gas place. What I remember is that most of the rooms had four or five beds in them, so if a band came over they could all stay in the same room. There was one room with just two beds in it, and Mick and I took that room every time. So we were both in that room that night.

There were plenty of lads in the hotel to hang out with, despite our late arrival. Seamus Shannon, a famous accordion player, was there, and so was the late Owen Shine, a brother of Brendan Shine. They were gigging, and they were both charmed that we were going to be on the television that week. The lads had a drink on our behalf. We stayed a while with them, but we didn't join them in the drink. We had an early night. We were exhausted and we had a long day ahead of us.

On Wednesday we headed to the BBC studio in Shepherd's Bush, getting there around ten o'clock. We were there all day. The BBC had their own way of doing things. You didn't play your instruments, but you had to sing live to a backing track. But to further complicate things, it wasn't your backing track you were playing to. The backing track was recorded that afternoon with the BBC's own band. So we brought our own producer Liam Hurley over with us. He knew our music, and was able to coordinate with the band to get the sound right. All the other bands had to do the same, so it was a busy few hours.

It was also an amazing few hours. There was great craic with the other bands, despite the fact that we were all so different. I remember that week there was Adam and the Ants, The Boomtown Rats from Dublin, Dexy's Midnight Runners, and a German band called the Goombay Dance Band. They were number one that week, with a song called 'Seven Tears'. We didn't really fit in with the Rats and the Ants, but we all mingled and enjoyed the craic.

We were just back from America and hadn't even had a chance to get to our homes, so we had to use what we had. And what we had were the *Barry Lyndon* costumes from the American tour. We put them on – black brogues with buckles, white knee socks, green pantaloons and jackets, and frilly white shirts. Bob Geldof, the lead singer of the Boomtown Rats, was very taken with the jackets. He had two saxophone players in his line-up, and he asked could he borrow the coats for them! I don't think they would have worn them.

After spending all afternoon getting the backing tracks right, and enjoying the craic in the green room, we were ready for the recording. That began at six o'clock. The show was filmed in a big square studio, packed with young people. It was very cleverly done. There was a stage set up against each of the four walls, and a band on each stage. So there was no mad scramble to clear the stage for the next act.

Because we weren't actually playing the music there was no need for Mick to take out his accordion. In fact it was suggested to us that it would look a bit off to bring an accordion onto *Top of the Pops*. So, we decided that both of us would strum a guitar, but we were in a pickle because we only had one. We contacted our good friend Seamus Moore, who within minutes arrived with another acoustic guitar for Mick. We were ready to go.

We stood still on the stage, taking it all in. Both of us were gripping our guitars, nervous under the heat of the lights. In front of us two hundred cheering young people milled around and danced. To one side, on a different stage, a band was going through its paces. Directly across the studio from us The Boomtown Rats were standing just like us, waiting.

There was no turning back now.

Before we knew it the presenter, Bruno Brookes, stood in front of the camera in a flecked grey jumper. He smiled and looked at the camera, then said: 'Here is a traditional song from Foster and Allen. They come from Westmeath in Ireland.'

As I sang I could see all the young people slowly revolving around each other in a poor man's semblance of a waltz. The floor was jammed. Then it was over, and back to the presenters and their countdown, before the next act was announced. The crowd would begin to dance again – this time a bit more wildly, because we were the mellowest of the acts. And just like that the biggest moment in our career to date was over, almost as quickly as it had begun.

While the attention was on the next stage we had a few minutes to get off, so that our stage could be used later in the show.

We were then surprised to see Dexy's Midnight Runners bring out an accordion – after we had been told it would not look right.

I looked at Mick and said, 'F**k sake!'

I suppose there is a lesson there: do what you feel is right, not what you are told.

The final act of the evening was that week's number one, the Goombay Dance Band. There were four of them, two fellows and two girls. I remember that one of the fellows, in a Hawaiian shirt that should have had its own volume control, had a flaming torch in his hand. He blew a great ball of flame over the crowd, then he stood up behind the microphone and began belting out their song. It was a memorable performance to say the least.

Then it was all over. It was like the plug had been pulled out, and all my energy suddenly drained away from me. Days of travel and jetlag, hours hanging around airports and studios, the adrenalin rush of it all, suddenly caught up on me and I was exhausted. It was a strange feeling, a mingling of relief that it was all over, and pride that it had gone so well. I looked over at Mick. I know that *Top of the Pops* meant very little to him as a rule, but I could see it in his face; he understood the enormity of this break. As the floor in front of us cleared, we smiled at one another, turned, and walked away.

I don't know what the craic was like after the performance. I presume some of them hung around and enjoyed the hospitality of the BBC for a few hours. Mick and I got into a taxi and rushed back to the airport for the last flight to Dublin. It was tight but we caught the nine o'clock flight and were in Dublin by ten. Then it was wearily home to Westmeath.

The next evening it would have been wonderful to sit in my own living room, stretched on the sofa, to enjoy the spectacle of two Westmeath lads on *Top of the Pops*. After seeing probably hundreds of episodes from my teens onwards, I had finally made it there myself.

But it was not to be. On Thursday evening we had a gig.

And so, instead of watching from the comfort of my own home, I got into a van with Mick and we drove up to Cavan. We were playing that night in the White Horse, a cabaret venue in Cootehill. After a long night's sleep we were back on the road.

We got to Cavan early and were able to watch our performance in the bar. Then we set up the gear and waited for our audience to arrive.

After the excitement of the previous evening's recording, it was a bit of an anti-climax. Only a handful of people showed up. We played to a nearly empty venue.

The reason was simple: the whole country knew we were on *Top of the Pops* that evening. So the people naturally assumed that we could hardly be in Cavan less than two hours later. They thought we would be no-shows. The innocence of it all – they did not understand the wonders of pre-recording.

It had been a crazy few days. Forty-eight hours had seen us in three countries, and on the most popular music show of the time, as well as playing to a tiny crowd in Cavan!

To this day I look back on those few days as one of the absolute highlights of our career.

'A Bunch of Thyme' didn't climb any higher in the charts, so number eighteen was its peak. But we were delighted with what it had already done for us. It had hit number one twice in Ireland, and was the third longest-staying single in the Irish charts behind Gloria's 'One Day at a Time' and Paddy Reilly's 'Fields of Athenry'. It was a massive forty weeks in the charts, as well as charting in the UK – and getting us the coveted *Top of the Pops* appearance. I had not been wrong when I had picked it out as a special song.

The one thing we weren't ready for was the terrible slagging we got for the suits we wore that night! We had been wearing them for seven years, up and down the country in every pub and parish hall, and on every television appearance, and no one took a blind bit of notice. Suddenly every newspaper in England was calling us the Leprechauns. We never intended to look like leprechauns. In fact, if you know what a leprechaun looked like, you'd know we weren't even close. It was typical eighteenth-century clothing, but they didn't see that.

Even the Irish media got in on it.

Did it bother us? Not in the slightest.

We had been dressing the same way for seven years. It was hardly going to bother us now.

We continued to play pubs and clubs around Ireland, and after *Top of the Pops* we were drawing a bigger crowd than ever. And when we returned to England our crowd had changed.

Now we weren't just playing to the ex-pats. English people were turning up. In fact, we had made the transition from niche act to mainstream act over there.

To this day when we tour England we are playing to English audiences more than the Irish community. What I like about that is that it means they are there because they love our music, not just because they are supporting some lads from home. The Irish community still support us, and we are delighted to see them as well.

Soon we were busier than ever back home. The *Top of the Pops* appearance was the cherry on top of the cake. We were moving to a new level of success.

We began touring concert venues in the UK for Ritz Records, sometimes for up to six weeks at a time, as well as touring extensively at home.

And that continued over the next year. Soon enough we were back in the recording studio, laying down more tracks. You can't rest on your laurels. We had a new producer at the time, Eamonn Campbell of The Dubliners.

We recorded 'Old Flames', which did well for us. It would have been too much to expect for it to be as big a hit as 'A Bunch of Thyme', and it wasn't. It peaked at fifty-one, which was solid, and it got plenty of airplay. 'Old Flames' was one of the most requested songs on the radio that year. Paschal Mooney, who had his *Keep it Country* show on RTÉ at the time, phoned us up to tell us that. Nothing was as popular with his listeners.

We also recorded 'Maggie'. We recorded it in the same session as 'Old Flames', but we released it later.

While I can take the credit for 'A Bunch of Thyme', I can't really take credit for 'Maggie'. Donie found the song for us. He mentioned it to me, and as you do when someone gives you a song title, you check it out.

I found a version by the Statler Brothers and loved it immediately. I could see where Donie was coming from.

So I called up Eamonn Campbell and played him the song over the phone. He liked the first verse, and asked me to give him a wee minute to see if he could tape it down the telephone.

As he was trying to do that, we got crossed wires, and a voice we did not know began singing along with the song! It gave us a laugh. So somewhere in Eamonn's archives there is a version of 'Maggie' accompanied by an unknown man in an unknown location singing his heart out.

Our producer liked the song, and it came out in March 1983, a year after 'A Bunch of Thyme' had been re-released. It charted high in Ireland, and was played off the air. RTÉ must have worn through a dozen copies of the record!

It also did very well in the UK, getting into the top thirty. We were put on alert for a return to *Top of the Pops* when it peaked at twenty-seven.

Would you believe it – we were back in America! There was no question of us flying home again. It was the middle of the tour this time. We couldn't let the people down. I was gutted: the previous appearance had been such a high point for me. But you have to take the good with the bad.

So our second appearance was a lot tamer than our first. We

continued our tour, while the BBC played a recording of 'Maggie'.

Videos were in their infancy back then. Most bands didn't make videos, and we certainly didn't. So while the song was playing they put up a picture. The picture they chose was the cover of the album, which featured a lovely dark-haired girl.

She smiled out at all the viewers while our song played.

Two years in a row the leprechauns had successfully invaded Shepherd's Bush.

CHAPTER TWENTY-ONE

FROM PUB HALLS TO CONCERT VENUES

MICK

Top of the Pops – despite the controversy of the suits – brought us to a new level entirely. We were no longer a cabaret act. Now we were bigger than that, and we had to think about how we would adapt to that new level of success.

The first thing we did was bring in a few lads to back us up. Dessie Hynes was on the keyboards, and Ollie Kennedy played bass. Both musicians came from the same band, Misty. When we were building a name on the cabaret circuit Misty had been one of the big acts, making money we could only dream of. But Misty broke up, leaving them at a loose end. They were both living in Mullingar, so I got in touch with them and asked them to join us. It gave us a fuller, richer sound.

When we brought in Dessie and Ollie we were now a concert band, pure and simple. You didn't need a four-piece to play a big pub – the economics of that made no sense. But we were a four-piece, and we were ready for the bigger venues. The dance halls were a dying thing by then, but every town had a theatre, every hotel had a large function room, and every village had a parish hall. There was no shortage of venues.

Just two hits had pushed us to the level of theatre shows. We were suddenly playing places that were far bigger than we were used to. We might be in a theatre tonight, and Cliff Richard might have been there last week with an orchestra. Ken Dodd might be there next week, with a band behind him. We had moved to that level. It got to the point that if we brought out a record and it didn't shift 300,000 copies, people would be wondering what was wrong. That gave us a serious thrill, but it also gave us a serious worry. As Foster and Allen we were just two lads with a keyboard and an accordion. Now we had to make it a show.

The addition of Dessie and Ollie helped a lot. There were more people on the stage and a bigger sound. We knew them both very well, which is why we hired them. They were veterans of the business. Both were top-class musicians. Dessie remained with us for eighteen years, before leaving to do his own thing. He still plays all over the country, as part of a two-piece. Ollie is still with us.

Over the years the band has expanded. Now there are five of us. When Dessie and Ollie joined, Tony went from the keyboard to the guitar. Dessie was a better keyboard player than Tony, but Tony had great drive at the instrument. To the punter in the audience Tony had been a great man on the keyboard because he gave it so much energy and drive. Now he is doing the same with the guitar. Tony can make it a show.

Expanding the band was something we did because we always wanted to give the public a great night. I suppose every band and entertainer does. So we tried to give that bit extra. You can do that with elaborate sets and fancy costumes, but in the end it is all about the music. And expanding our line-up made us sound great.

Our next idea was to have strong support acts. That way someone would have plenty of variety, and would get value for their ticket. This was particularly important when we toured the UK. At the time there was a strong market for Irish acts, and for our early UK tours when we were beginning to taste success, we brought along very strong support acts. We began as we meant to continue, hiring the best. For our first concert tour in the UK we were supported by two acts. TR Dallas and his band opened the show; Tom Allen had become a big draw in his own right, with his Stetson hat and humorous lyrics. It was good to be back on the road with him. Philomena Begley and her band closed the first half of the show. She was a huge country star. They did half an hour each, and both acts had a full band.

Then we came on – the two of us, with just two men behind us! But it was obvious that people were enjoying our music, so that was not a problem. Concerts were so much easier than pub gigs. For a start, we were only doing an hour. It felt awfully handy, after being used to two hours or more in a pub. The second big difference was in the attitude and attention of the audience.

In a pub, as soon as you open your mouth to sing, you are in a row straight away with Arthur Guinness. People are in the pub to have a drink and a chat. If you turn up the volume, they will talk all the louder. In a pub, half the audience are there because they wanted to go to the pub to have a drink. Of what is left, half might be your fans, and half might be there just to check you out, out of curiosity. But in a theatre, everyone is there to see you. Nobody just comes along for the sake of it. Nobody has stopped by to have a pint on the way to the races, or to unwind after a stressful day at work. They have paid for the tickets, and they actually want to hear you. That is a big difference.

Those early concert tours were such easy work. We were all travelling together on a coach, and it was great craic. There were a bunch of us together, all in our late twenties or early thirties, all with similar interests and ambitions. How could that not be fun? We were earning enough so that we did not have to rush home every night to save the shillings. We stayed over every night, unless we were very close to home.

Neither Tony nor I were great drinkers. Some of the lads touring with us were drinkers, but it never got out of hand. However much fun it was, it was work. Business was always first, and every lad was up in the morning for their breakfast, and ready for the road. There was never any danger of a lad not turning up. We left the wild rock-and-roll lifestyle to others!

Over the next few years we tried different types of support act, constantly looking for quality. We have toured with Louise Morrissey, Philomena Begley and Sean Cuddy. We have experimented with unusual support acts that are a sharp contrast to us – trumpeters, comedians, we even used a comedy magician for a while. One year we tried to do a full show, not just ourselves and a support act. We had some great acts, from all over.

But gradually the message from our fans sank in. They were coming to see us, not the support act. No matter who we used, someone would crib. In the end we thought, why bother? We had believed that a full show with plenty of variety would be a better job, but our audience didn't look at it that way. At the end of the day they wanted to see us, and that was it. So for the past fifteen years we have not used any support acts. It is just ourselves and our band. We do a full two-hour show again like the old pub days. With one difference – there is no row with Arthur Guinness!

The only time we will use a support act now is on a foreign tour. In Australia on our next tour there are two dates that we will be doing double shows. Rather than perform for four hours and be exhausted the following day, we will have a support act those days. They will open the show, and we will do a second half of an hour and twenty minutes.

Concert tours, at least at home, were never seven nights a week, like the old cabaret days. It was never as busy. You do fewer shows but they are bigger shows, for a bigger fee. These days our tours of Ireland tend to involve us doing shows from Thursday through to Sunday, then taking a few days off. We keep that up for five weeks. Monday, Tuesday and Wednesday are not great days for drawing a crowd, so we don't try. In a five-week tour we can hit twenty venues, and we go for places that we can fill.

Nowadays there is a theatre in almost every town. We do some great ones, such as the Cork Opera House. It is modern, with a top-class sound system and great acoustics. It fits a thousand or more, yet everyone seems almost close enough to touch. The Concert Hall in the University of Limerick is the same. But we also play a lot of hotels. That is a business decision. Some theatres charge an arm and a leg. Hotels tend to be more reasonable. In a good hotel with a large function room, you can fit 1,200 people. They have ample parking, and people can have a drink before the show starts.

We still play theatres in Northern Ireland, and the occasional one down south. But hotels are taking over. It is important to get a local radio station on board at every gig. If they get involved in the promotion they will blast it off the air for weeks beforehand, ensuring we draw a good crowd. Before we did those deals we would be trying to negotiate the best advertising deal with them, and fighting for everything. Now they are part of the action, and it works out better for everyone. Those are the tricks you learn as you go along; playing the music is the easy part. Of course, it is also the fun part. And all our decisions, then and now, are designed to ensure that we have a good enthusiastic crowd to play to.

When we began to play the concert venues, around 1982 and '83, I constantly had to pinch myself to remind me it was all real. It was so easy compared to the cabaret days. It didn't feel like work. If the crowd are with you – and they had to be, because they bought the tickets – they were a pleasure to play for. They sat there and listened, and clapped along, and laughed at our bits of banter between the songs. We were all in it together, and you'd feel great walking off the stage.

Tony and I began to manage ourselves once more around that time. It is a quirk of our personalities; we like to be in control of things. But we were very grateful to Donie Cassidy for all he had done, and we remain great friends with him.

In fact, to this day he is still the man we record for. And his son Peter has followed him into the business. We work very closely with the two of them. Tony and I will tell Peter what dates we want to tour from, and Peter sets up the venues for us. He is our promoter. And we could not have done better with anyone else. Not even Louis Walsh or Simon Cowell!

We have been working with the Cassidys since 1978, and we will continue to work with them – even though we managed ourselves once more from the early eighties onwards.

Why would we break up a winning team?

CHAPTER TWENTY-TWO

ONWARDS AND UPWARDS

TONY

We so enjoyed the new level of success that *Top of the Pops* had opened up for us. But as we moved from being a cabaret act to a concert act, we had to adapt and change to our new status.

It was a big step up. There was an upside and a downside. The upside was that you were playing bigger venues for better money, so you could play less of them. The audience were there to hear you, rather than being there for the drink. So that made life easier. The downside was that you needed a bigger, showier, act. You had to make an impact and an impression in a large venue in a way that just wasn't the same as in a cabaret lounge. We had to work on that, to make sure the audience came away satisfied.

We had done concerts before *Top of the Pops*. You would get the odd call to do one somewhere. But after our two appearances on that flagship show, the calls were getting more frequent. By 1983 we were playing concerts regularly. We were drawing crowds. We had always done well, but all of a sudden the doors would have to be closed half an hour before the show because the place was stuffed. That changed things. We were getting calls to do concerts in village halls and community centres, so we had to get a bigger PA system. The 200-watt Dynacord just wasn't enough any more. Not once we brought in Dessie and Ollie.

I suddenly found myself moving out from the keyboard, which was a change. I had been playing the keyboard for seven years. Now I had to get used to the guitar again. But I had been playing the guitar since my early teens. It was the first instrument I was any good at, and I loved it. I had played it on *Top of the Pops*, and it was the instrument I had used for my first-ever public performance. So the adjustment was easily made. In one sense there was no great difference. I was still playing an instrument, and still singing.

Mick was always the better man at chatting to an audience. My strength was in communicating through the music. I love a good song, and over the years we have been lucky enough to record and perform some great ones. The concert halls were great venues for those songs.

While I was making my adjustments to our new status, the band as a whole was facing its own concerns. For a start, what would we wear on stage? For seven years we had worn the same costumes, the *Barry Lyndon* suits that everyone mistakenly called the leprechaun suits. After *Top of the Pops* we were typecast as the singing wee folk. But if the lads were backing us, they would have to be dressed the same as us. We gave it some thought, and decided the time had come to ditch the costumes and wear suits. We had outgrown the green costumes, after all these years.

Dessie and Ollie added a great deal to the richness of the Foster and Allen sound. We were still a two-piece out front, and they were backing us beautifully. It worked very well; they filled the stage and made us look more like a concert act, as well as making our sound fuller and more varied.

At that stage we were still our own roadies, with occasional help. Our army buddy Tommy Cussen came along with us whenever he was free, and he sold records in the lobby as well as helping with the gear. He was a great lad to have around. It was a terrible blow to us when he and his son were killed in a tragic road accident, just as we were beginning to taste success. We didn't just lose a useful man; we lost a good friend. His wife moved to England, and we still meet up with her when we are on tour over there.

The loss of Tommy knocked us back; he was such a young man. But we had to carry on.

Every concert began with a mad scramble to bring in speakers and amps and wire them all up. The equipment was a lot simpler than it is today – you didn't need an engineering degree just to switch it on. At the end of every show we would wait until the venue was clearing out a bit and then get stuck into packing everything away, and getting it all back in the van for the trip home.

But the operation was getting bigger. With four on the road we had more equipment. And with bigger halls to play we had to get bigger amps and speakers.

Then people started asking us for autographs. So after the show Mick and I would go out and meet the audience. We'd shake hands, pose for photographs, chat with them and sign all the scraps of paper that were pushed in front of us. That took a while, and by the end of it we wouldn't be in fit form for pulling down gear. And it could be getting late.

So eventually we bowed to the inevitable, and took on someone to go on the road with us, to put up the gear and look after that side of things. The first man we took on was Johnny Moran, the original drummer with The Marylanders. He became our first roadie.

But no matter how late a night ran, we would always head for home in the evening. We never stayed away. Mick had been married for a number of years, and I also got married. We both wanted to be home in our own beds at the end of our working day. I wanted to see my two small boys. Sadly my marriage did not work out, but we were blessed with two fine lads that I am very proud of. They are both in their early thirties now. Ian is married to Sutanya, and they have presented us with two beautiful grandchildren, Surin-Rose and Ava. Keith, a year younger, is living in London. He plays music – which I suppose is no surprise! They are two great lads who have been nothing but a joy to us.

Luckily Ireland is a small country, which made getting home possible. We'd be finished most nights by half-eleven or twelve, and we would be back in Westmeath in a few hours. Even if we were doing a concert as far away as Skibbereen in West Cork we would try to get back. Dawn might have broken, but we would put our heads down on our own pillows.

It was also a change having a bunch of us in the van. For years it had just been Mick and me. We were a strange pair. We could go for miles without saying a word to each other. We could get into the van and drive the whole way to Limerick without opening our mouths. There was no point, if we had nothing to say. But there was never a bad word between us, and never an argument in all the years we have been together. So it was a companionable silence. At Easter we might buy a box of Caffrey's chocolate mallows and throw them between us in the van. They wouldn't last long. We both had a sweet tooth. We were always hungry, but we weren't putting on weight at that stage because we were young.

With four or five of us on the road together, though, a box of mallows wouldn't last long! That was one of the prices of success!

As we were moving towards being a concert act rather than a cabaret act we had to put more thought into our programme. The pubs had been easy. You would just play for two hours – and maybe take a few minutes break in the middle. You would play a few good lively numbers that would get them up on the floor, and maybe a few of the songs that were big at the moment. You would end on the National Anthem, load up and go home.

For a concert you needed to do a bit more planning. In our early days, as Mick has said, we would do concerts with other acts. We would have someone play the first half, and we would do the second half. We used all sorts of acts – strong country bands, instrumentalists, good singers. We even experimented with comedians and magicians to open for us. But we always did an hour and a half to two hours ourselves. If an audience came to see us we would make sure they got their value.

However, soon enough we began doing the shows on our own, and the programme became even more important, as we were the variety and it was down to us and us alone to provide an evening of entertainment such as our fans were looking for. The programme would be made up of a mix of songs and tunes. Mick and I put the programme together, both of us contributing ideas and suggestions, and in all the years we have never had an argument over it.

That said, there are differences in what we like. Mick loves his trad, and we always include some jigs and reels – purely instrumental pieces – that showcase his talent on the accordion. I am a stronger singer, and so we always include some of the songs I love. Mick sings the odd comic song, and the audience always enjoy those, so we throw a couple of them into the mix. In truth it wasn't very difficult to put together a programme that suited both us and our audience.

Occasionally we get it wrong; a song won't work for us. But then we would switch it for something else the next night. That was the joy of us managing ourselves and being in control – we could just change things if it was clear they weren't working, and we weren't beholden to anyone.

And in practice, on the whole, the songs balanced out. The programme was designed to suit the audience rather than ourselves. But it was a no-brainer, because we liked what the audience liked.

Another consequence of success was that people offered us songs. Our bass player Ollie wrote a lovely song with Ber Coleman, and we began to play that. 'After All These Years' proved very popular with our audiences, and after we recorded it in 1985, it became a perennial favourite. It is probably the most requested song we ever recorded. We would not dream of doing a concert without singing it.

Within a year of switching to the concert circuit we were very busy. Although the venues we were playing were new to us, the towns we were visiting were not. We had been playing the cabaret lounges in them only months previously. So we had a dedicated fan base to play to everywhere we went.

And the gigs weren't the only developments in our career. We were recording albums alongside our performances, and our recording output was becoming really successful – we were even beginning to chart outside of Ireland. Things were starting to take off for us on an international scale. So then we had to consider making the leap to tour abroad. And not just the Irish circuit in the States or a little week-long tour on a small scale in the UK – we were talking a proper tour with us as headliners and a loyal audience to please.

Exciting times were looming for us, far beyond our native shores.

CHAPTER TWENTY-THREE

CARRYING OUT OUR TRADE

MICK

By the mid-eighties we were doing better than we could ever have dreamed. Donie Cassidy played a big part in that early success. He may not have been managing us any more, but that didn't mean we weren't benefitting from his influence and support, and we were still reaping the rewards of the things he had done for us as our manager. The management thing was just a personal choice for Tony and me, because we both like to be in control of what we are doing. We don't like a lad telling us we are in Cork tonight and Donegal tomorrow – which a manager would do. As long as they are filling the diary and making money it doesn't matter to them that they are sitting on their arse in an office and we are driving madly around the country. But it mattered to us.

But in fairness, nothing would have happened without Donie. Our success might have happened to an extent, but not to the scale he was able to achieve for us. It is very hard for an ordinary Joe Soap to get on the radio and television with any regularity. You have to be in the know. We gobshites wouldn't have been in the know at all, but Donie was. He had the contacts to get us exposure, and to move us along. When he started we were on £100 a night. Very quickly – almost immediately – he was able to jump that to £500 a night. That was big money back then, leaving us very comfortable. And it didn't end there.

Our first proper tour of England in the mid-eighties was mighty. Both of us had been there before of course, with The Nightrunners and other bands, but they had been small tours, just a weekend or a week. Ten days would have been the most we would have done before that. Now we were a concert act. We were staying there for a month or more and playing the bigger venues.

The first big change was that we weren't driving a van. We were being driven, in a tour bus. It was always tour busses in the UK. They were fabulous coaches with everything you could have wanted. They were fitted out for comfort. There was a sleeping area if you wanted it, and a lounge with a television and a video machine, so that you could sit down and watch a movie. There was a kitchen where you could make a cup of tea or a sandwich, and there were plenty of comfortable couches and chairs.

We had nothing to worry about. There was a tour manager looking after us, and a driver driving the bus. There was nothing for us to do but sit back and relax. Which we were more than happy to do. It was so much more fun than tearing around the highways and byways of Ireland in the red Hiace.

It was a great way to travel. When we started in the mid-seventies we were going around bad roads in a banger of a van, with the cold air whistling through the strained door. Now we were on a motorway in a luxury coach. It was heavenly.

There would always be craic on the tour bus. None of us were wild men. We were country gawks for want of a better word. But we enjoyed what life had to offer us. We could sit around and chat, or break open a deck of cards. A couple of us might sit down and watch a film. Of if you wanted peace you could find a comfortable chair and read a book, or go down to the sleeping quarters and catch up on forty winks. There was plenty of space, so there was never a danger of us getting on one another's nerves.

In the early years of our success we used to spend April in the UK, then return in November. In the month we might do twenty-five shows. Today we do one tour, of about a month's duration. It is the same with Australia. As young men we would go out there every eighteen months – more on that later. But now, we go every two or sometimes three years. You slow down with age. We have been close to forty years on the road as Foster and Allen, and sometimes we think it is a wonder that anyone wants to listen to us still. They have heard us, their children have heard us, and sometimes their grandchildren have heard us. But they do still want to hear us, and we are delighted with that. We still tour four months of the year, and we still enjoy it.

Touring the UK we tend to do one set of theatres this time, and a different set the next time. So if we play Liverpool this year, we will skip it the next. That way when we come back they still want us. We have travelled the whole country, from Inverness right down to Truro in Cornwall, from Great Yarmouth across to Liverpool and into Wales.

We used different promoters over the years. We started with Ritz Records; they were the ones who pushed us up the charts and onto *Top of the Pops*. They organised our first tours. Then they stopped touring, and handed us over to Dolphin Promotions. Dudley Russell was the man in charge then. Dudley was married to the comic poet Pam Ayres, who was on television quite a lot back then. He handled our tours for quite a number of years. We went from him to Bill Delaney, a Scottish man living in London. After Bill, Robert Pratt of Chimes International took over. He was the personal manager of Don Williams, the American singer/songwriter. We toured for Robert for years and

years. We had the same tour manager, Jim Hughes, for all those
years, which helped things run smoothly. Now, Peter Cassidy,
from CMR Records here in Ireland, is handling our UK tours.
This is his first year doing that, and we are looking forward to
seeing how he handles it.

For decades David Hull Promotions, based in Belfast, handled
all our Irish tours. We worked with him from the late eighties to
last year, and he was a very straight man, and very hard-
working. We worked very well together over the years, travelling
the length and breadth of Ireland. He organised all the venues
around the country.

We got on great with all the tour promoters. We never gave
them problems, and they never gave us problems. If a tour
manager said that we had to be ready to leave at five, then
everyone would be in the hotel lobby at ten to five, bags packed
and ready to move. There was no such thing as a lad stumbling
down the stairs at five past five. We made sure never to give
them any problems.

In fairness they treated us the same way – they were all a
pleasure to work with.

When you look back the tours have their highs and lows. But
they also have a sense of routine about them. We were working
men carrying out our trade. It is the early tours that stand out
because it was all so new to us in the eighties. We were seeing
places for the first time. We were seeing our music spread
through the world. The mid-eighties were good days for us.

And they were about to get even better.

CHAPTER TWENTY-FOUR

TOURING AUSSIE-STYLE

TONY

I had been to the UK with a number of bands, and I had even been as far as America with Foster and Allen. But now the whole world was about to open out for us. The birth of those international touring days began in France – and we weren't even there!

Every year there is a huge trade event for the music industry in the glamorous town of Cannes. MIDEM has been running since 1967, and industry heads from all over the world come there to check out what's new. A representative from our record company in London had brought our single 'Maggie' to the fair back in 1983, and it was one of the tracks buyers from other parts of the world were listening to.

To our happy surprise, an Australian record company called Powderworks picked it up for the Australian market. They had picked up 'Sweet Sixteen' the year before. They went for that sort of material quicker than rock acts, because that is what the Australian market was looking for. 'Maggie' became a huge hit in Australia.

When we started to hear about our success overseas we were over the moon. People on the far side of the world were listening to us. If you stop to think about it, that is amazing. But we were too busy to stop and think about it. We had a busy touring schedule at home and in the UK.

Bit by bit, our music began to go on sale in Australia, New Zealand, Canada, the USA and South Africa, and began to do well. You don't obsessively watch the charts in other countries, so it snuck up on us. Almost before we realised what was happening, we had become major stars in those countries, so inevitably there was demand for us to visit them. It began with Australia. Sometimes chance plays a part in your success, and it certainly did in that country; chance, and a dedicated team of record-company pluggers.

Pluggers are the people who are on the road for the record companies. They are part sales rep, part PR manager. They will arrive in a town and call into the record stores to make sure that your album is displayed to the best advantage. They will chat to the staff, and if they make a good impression the staff might push one record above another. Then they will visit the local newspaper and chat to the music and entertainment journalists. In a country like Australia there were plenty of local radio stations, and they would visit these, to talk to the DJs and presenters.

The single was flying off the shelves. The record company executive, Ken Harding, sat up and took notice. They began to push it properly throughout the country, and before we knew it, 'Maggie' was at number one. Number one! 'Maggie' spent five weeks in the top spot.

As I said, the success crept up on us!

'Maggie' also reached number one in New Zealand for five weeks, and we were blown away by how successful it had been internationally.

Two Australian promoters were quick to see the opportunity. John Nicholls and Adrian Bohm invited us out to tour there.

Australia was so far away I hadn't even considered visiting there before that, but it was a great opportunity, and of course we said yes.

So one chilly November day in 1983, we left Dublin for the long haul to the other side of the world. We were escaping the cold and wet of Ireland for the southern summer. We were guaranteed sunny skies, bright days and full houses. Our first tours of England had been to play to the ex-pats in Irish clubs and pubs. America was the same – we were playing to our own. But in Australia we were coming over as a number-one act, and it was a concert tour. This was the real thing. The sense of excitement was tremendous.

To put it in context, imagine an Australian act that was number one over here – think of the reception they would get. There was a huge crowd waiting for us when we touched down on Australian soil. As the door of the plane opened the blast of hot air hit us. Both of us had been to the sun before, but this was a new type of heat! It was all part of the exoticness of the experience.

We got into the airport, and were amazed by the crowds there to greet us. They even had a piper to pipe us through the terminal. Then the promoter had a big car waiting to take the five of us – Mick, myself, Ollie, Dessie and our road manager, Johnny Moran – to the first hotel of our tour.

Then it was straight into a crazy round of radio and television appearances. We were in multi-channel land, so we were pulled every which way. That was an absolutely brilliant experience. There was a great media buzz around us. We were new so we were a novelty, and the welcome mat was thrown out for us. We threw ourselves into the publicity whirlwind. We were invited to appear on radio and television shows, and we did them all. There was a great sense of excitement about it. Of course, being a vast country there were plenty of radio and television stations, unlike Ireland, with just one of each at the time. So that meant that each appearance had less impact. But we did so many it made up for that!

During those eight weeks we worked almost every day. We got the occasional day off – perhaps one every week or week and a half. But apart from that it was all go. Sometimes we did double shows on the same day. But it wasn't as hectic as it sounded. The Australian Musician's Union had a rule. When a foreign act was touring, they had to be supported by a local act. And for every outside musician employed one local had to get the gig. There were four of us on stage, so we were always supported by at least a four-piece. It was a condition of getting our visa.

We would do an hour and twenty minutes to an hour and a half, which felt easy. Because of the support acts we could afford to do the double gigs without exhausting ourselves.

Now when we tour Australia we have our own sound engineer with us. But on that first visit the tour promoter provided the sound engineer, Mark Wilkinson. For the stage crew we used local guys. So there were just the five of us travelling each day. But there were no luxury coaches laid on. The five of us would bundle into a minibus or a large people carrier. No television, no kettle – but the craic was still great. We had no complaints about being chauffeured around Australia in big luxury cars – but it would have been nice if they could have built the towns a bit closer to each other. There were endless hours of long straight motorway, with flat, arid scenery stretching miles in every direction.

The tour had been carefully planned, and we made a steady progression around the country. We played neighbouring cities so we never had to travel more than a few hours each day, or every second day if we were doing a few nights in the one place.

Because our chart success made us a big-name act we were the equivalent of a pop band. We were playing all the big venues. We played the National Concert Hall in Melbourne two nights in a row. We were seven or eight nights in The

Gold Coast. This is the Australian equivalent of Las Vegas – all the big acts play there. When the venue was opened originally, Frank Sinatra was the first act. You could say he warmed up the place for us! We played Perth, Brisbane, all the cities. Many of the places we did three or four nights in a row.

One of the most amazing memories was playing the Sydney Opera House, because it is such an iconic venue. It was brilliant to play it, but a very strange experience at the same time. It was huge – and there were so many steps up to it. And we filled it. That was some thrill, to fill the Sydney Opera House. I near enough had to pinch myself to remind myself it really was happening. But I knew we were number one, so I should have been prepared for the madness.

Walking out in front of three thousand people was a new experience for us. But we had been playing big theatres in the UK, venues that fitted 1,500 to 2,000 people. This was bigger again, but we were young and full of energy, and we were ready for it.

The first time you step in front of a new audience in a new territory of course you are nervous. You wonder if you will go down well. So there were nerves those first few gigs in Australia. But they quickly settled. After so many years on the road the nerves don't affect you nearly as badly. Looking out over crowds all over the globe we have come to a realisation; all Foster and Allen audiences are the consistent the world over.

Of course, they are not *all* the same. They come from different walks of life, and different backgrounds. What I mean is that they are consistent. They have two very important things in common: they know our music and they are there for us. So whether it is Perth or Preston or Portlaoise, we know that they are going to enjoy the show.

Personally I prefer audiences of four or five hundred, because you are closer to everyone, and it is a lot nicer to work an audience that size. I am sure the promoter would prefer 10,000 but for me as an artist I like a small theatre that is full. That is magic. Nevertheless, I took the big Australian audiences in my stride.

The Australians are a warm and friendly people and I liked them enormously. About the only downside was being so far away from home. I missed my family.

But there was always a good phone system, even in the eighties. I would ring home every day. I am sure Mick was doing the same. Today is no different, except we have mobile phones. Back then we had to wait until we got to the next hotel. But it wasn't that inconvenient.

As long as conditions are right, life on the road is not a bad life. I'm a very basic steak and chips man, and I want a good breakfast. And any place Foster and Allen have ever toured you can get that. We stay in very good hotels. You can get Chinese and Indian food everywhere in the world. We aren't fussy. None of the band is. In the hotels we always have a room to ourselves. That is important – you need time on your own, and a bit of privacy, to keep sane. If you had to look at the same face for twenty-four hours a day, seven days a week, there is no knowing what you might end up doing, even to someone you like a lot.

Life on the road falls into a rhythm. We would get up in the morning and have our breakfast, then it was into the car for a few hours before checking into the next hotel. We would check in around two or three o'clock – which was generally in time for lunch.

I didn't take much time out for sightseeing. I might walk down to a shop or a supermarket just to look around but I wasn't interested beyond that. Some people look at touring as a glamorous life, but you are working. There are sound checks and rehearsals and television and radio interviews. It is not a holiday.

I brought my son Keith to Australia one year for a tour, and that was lovely. He was in his teens, and it was great to have his company, and what father doesn't enjoy travelling with his child? But it didn't change the format. I still did the sound check at five, the show at seven-thirty, finish at ten, then back to the hotel. Sometimes we would vary it by heading out for a bite to eat after the concert. Then we would get up the next morning at eight o'clock, have our breakfast and head off again. It is like any man's day of work.

As I said, it is work – but what work! The thrill of standing in front of a crowd, and they loving your music, is indescribable. Since that first Australian tour we have been back eighteen times, sometimes for as long as eight weeks. You work hard on those tours. But it can still be fun. You don't go out there to see the country, but inevitably you do see bits. We have been there so often now that I think I have seen everything worth seeing!

The first time we went out we were taken out by a promoter called Adrian Bohm. We have watched his family grow up over the years. His wife Veronica is the company secretary. His son Seb was a small baby back then. Now he works alongside his father in their business. He has three girls, who all work in the business. It is still Adrian whom we tour for, and it is great to arrive and see a familiar and friendly face waiting for you.

Our Australian tour manager has remained the same through all the years as well. He is Michael Hayes. We have seen his children growing up too. You can't underestimate the importance of a good tour manager, and Michael is one of the best. When you arrive at the far side of the world it is a comfort to see a familiar and friendly face.

We have also become close to the record company executive behind our success, Ken Harding. Ken, along with his wife Margaret, still handles all of Foster and Allen's records in Australia.

After so many years of working together we have grown very friendly with the Hardings. They came over to see Ireland a few years ago, and we looked after them. Margaret did not believe that the mountains of Mourne swept down to the sea, as the Percy French song says. So we brought her up there and put her in a good hotel so that she could see for herself!

CHAPTER TWENTY-FIVE

THE ICE RINK

MICK

Our international success seemed to just keep on growing. Another of the places where we were an unexpected hit was in Nova Scotia and Newfoundland on the west of Canada. Our albums and singles never did very well in North America, and when we played there, it was to the ex-pat community. But Nova Scotia was an exception. By a quirk we became stars there. We played our biggest-ever audience at a gig in the small town of Sydney, Nova Scotia.

Our very first visit to Canada came at the invitation of businessman Pat Quinn. Pat was a real entrepreneur, from Leitrim. He had started as a music promoter in the sixties, and it was through the music business he met his wife Anne – in our own Roseland Ballroom. They honeymooned in Toronto, and then he went there to live. He promoted shows by The Beach Boys, Johnny Cash, Roy Orbison and The Supremes. He was the first promoter to introduce the Rolling Stones to North America.

Then he returned to Ireland and set up Quinnsworth, a nationwide chain of supermarkets. He eventually sold on the chain and became a very rich man. Now they are owned by Tesco. But Pat was never one to confine himself to one venture. He had many interests. In the eighties he returned to Toronto for good, where he became involved in the hospitality business, and he also continued to dabble in promotion.

So it was Pat who brought us to Toronto, where we did a few shows. Although Pat has sadly passed on now, his family still give us a great welcome whenever we go to Canada. The pubs he established are still a home away from home for any touring Irish musician.

Then a man in Nova Scotia, Norman Leadbetter, began to show an interest in one of our singles. Norman owned a record shop, and he had a show on the local radio station. The song he was taken with was 'I Will Love You All of My Life'. He began to play it and to push it, and it became a huge success in Nova Scotia, a province on the Atlantic coast of Canada.

The song was such a success there that Norman decided to ask us out to play. Our first trip to Nova Scotia was in 1984, a few months after coming home from our first tour of Australia. While down under we had played Sydney, and now we were playing Sydney again. But this time it was Sydney, Nova Scotia. Sydney is by no means the biggest city in the province. It has a population of just 31,000, making it only a bit bigger than Ennis, a good market town in Ireland. But we filled the theatre five nights in a row. We did Monday to Friday, and I remember on Saturday night Liam Clancy and Tommy Makem were in the same venue.

The following year Norman got us back out again, and this time he was more ambitious. If we could fill a theatre five nights in a row, imagine what we could do with just one night, well promoted? A town that size, of course, did not have any big venues. But he used a bit of ingenuity. He got us to play in the local ice rink!

We couldn't believe it when we arrived. He had set up a stage at one end of the rink, and the audience filled the seats and spilled out onto where the ice would normally be. He had put in a temporary floor to accommodate the seating. We had a serious sound system in place – we had to, to fill that space. We were ready well in advance, as usual. We sat there behind the scenes and watched in amazement as the most people we had ever seen at one of our concerts filtered in and took their seats. By the end there were 6,500 people in the rink, and all there to see us. To put that in an Irish context, it was the equivalent of filling the Royal Albert Hall or the Point Depot, if the Point Depot had been in Ennis! It was a massive crowd.

We were at the far end of the rink, which might not have been the best idea. Maybe we should have been in the centre, so that everyone could see us. But it was an incredible experience. When you come from playing small pubs, and playing venues such as The Brazen Head in Limerick to twelve people on Christmas Eve just a few short years earlier, it is boost to your ego to be playing for more than six thousand. It was great to have that many people come specially to hear us, especially on the other side of the world. We weren't part of any show or festival. It was just us. That was great.

The show went very well. They all enjoyed themselves. But as I looked out I kept thinking of the people from the middle of the rink back. We must have seemed like ants to them, we were so far away!

The next time we returned to Nova Scotia we played the ice rink again. But this time we split it into two nights, and only used half the rink. That made the shows more intimate. They were still huge events, but at least everyone could spot us on the stage! We also played Halifax, the capital of Nova Scotia.

Then a promoter called Leo Puddester brought us out to Newfoundland, further north up the coast of Canada. We played in Newfoundland and Labrador City. We have also returned to Toronto. But we have never travelled any further

west than that. To us a tour of Canada is Nova Scotia and
Newfoundland. We still go out there regularly.

But nothing beats the memory of that second tour, and the
biggest crowd who have ever turned up just to see us.

We have played bigger crowds in our career, but always at big
events. We sang at half-time in an All-Ireland football final
before 80,000 people, and we have played at the Cleveland Folk
Festival and the Roundwood Park Irish Festival in London, both
of which draw massive crowds. But this was different. In Nova
Scotia they were there for us, not because there was an event
on. Every one of those 6,500 people had bought a ticket to
see Foster and Allen. It was an incredible feeling. It gave us a
brief taste of what the big stadium acts must experience night
after night.

Normally big crowds are less of a buzz than you would
imagine. At the big festivals no one is there for you specifically.
There could be 70,000 people at Roundwood Park in London,
and a similar crowd in Cleveland, Ohio. But they wouldn't all be
watching you. There would be six stages. We could be
performing on a stage at one end of the park, and further up
the field there would be The Dubliners, Johnny McEvoy might
be somewhere else, and Paddy Reilly on yet another stage. The
lineout might be completed with a ceili band or two. It was
madness.

People were there for the craic and they might not be
interested in what you were doing. They might come and sit
down and listen for ten minutes, then get up again and move on
to the next stage. You played for an hour, then the next act took
over. Over the weekend you would play to a serious number of
people, but you were making no real connection with most of
them. It was an event rather than a concert.

It was all out in the open, and there wasn't a hope of making
it feel like a real show. People drifted around, with the hardcore
fans staying near the front. As a performer there is not the same

buzz from those festivals, despite the numbers. But it was great to take part in them.

And there were unexpected bonuses.

One thing I loved was that you were mingling with the other performers, and some of them were legends in the business. I had always been a huge fan of the late Tommy Makem. Our first few albums always had a Makem song on them. At those festivals I got to meet people like him, and that was a huge buzz. We eventually became great friends. Whenever he came to Ireland on tour he called to my house for three or four hours. We would chat and walk the locality. He was a great man for history and folklore and we have plenty of that in this neck of the woods.

It was a privilege to get to meet these people – people you would have admired as a youngster growing up – and to get to know them as well as you might know a lad down the road. Without the big festivals, that would never have happened.

CHAPTER TWENTY-SIX

THE MOST CONTROVERSIAL BAND IN IRELAND

TONY

After successful tours in Australia and Canada, we got the chance to tour South Africa – and that landed us in hot water, to say the least.

If you had to pick a band in Ireland least likely to be at the centre of a storm of controversy, it would be Foster and Allen. We are not wild rockers. You won't hear of us off our heads on drugs or trashing hotel rooms. We are the safe face of the music world. But in 1985 we became the most controversial music act in Ireland when we accepted the invitation to tour South Africa.

We weren't looking at the bigger picture. To us at that time South Africa was just another territory where someone was trying to sell our music. And they were doing a good job of it, because we were charting there. People were buying our records and we were becoming quite popular. The record was playing off the air. We had several albums in the charts down there, not just the single, 'Maggie' – which had reached number one. The record company wanted us out there, and that was our job.

We were honestly not aware of what a big stir it would cause.

You have to understand that South Africa was not something that was on the consciousness of many Irish people at that time. Awareness came later. At the time South Africa operated a system called apartheid, where the white minority controlled the country, and the black majority were denied civil rights. The international community responded with cultural and sporting boycotts of the country. But despite the involvement of the UN with the boycotts, many ordinary people were not aware of the situation at that time. We certainly weren't.

So when a promoter from South Africa, Ronnie Quibell, approached our management and invited us to perform there, we agreed. Ronnie, who passed away in 2012, was an interesting guy. He was a theatrical and music promoter who broke ranks with all the others by insisting that his performances were mixed. None of his shows were segregated. And he had clashed with the authorities by bringing over black artists such as Eartha Kitt. Some of them had used their performances as a political platform and had been thrown back out of the country! In his own way Ronnie was doing his best to battle the apartheid system.

My – perhaps naive – feeling was that there were a lot of people there who bought our music, and they were entitled to hear us. And they certainly weren't going to travel over here just for that. And our shows absolutely weren't segregated; everyone was welcome, no matter what their colour or background.

That tour was crazily busy. It was Australia all over again. We were there for over a month, and we did forty-two gigs that month. It was a hectic schedule. When we finally arrived home we were totally unprepared for the controversy our trip had provoked. There were letters to the papers and editorials slamming us. It wasn't like we were the only Irish gigs to go out there, but for some reason we seemed to get the flak.

I remember there were even protests at some of our concerts. We would look down from the stage and see banners being waved from the front row. It was very unpleasant. We weren't happy about it, but what could we do? We also heard that there were protests in Australia and New Zealand. It was hard. Nobody likes to be disliked. We are entertainers – our job is to spread happiness, not discord.

We went and visited Kader Asmal, the leader of the Irish Anti-Apartheid Movement. We sat down in his office and discussed the whole thing. We explained that no one had raised any objections before we went out. There were no letters, no protests, no approaches from the Anti-Apartheid Movement. I don't think Kader Asmal even knew who we were beforehand. All the protests had come after the event, when it was too late to do anything about it.

I thought the meeting went well. We assured him that we were now fully aware of the political situation and the implications of our visit, and we would not tour South Africa again while apartheid was in place. And we kept our word: we did not return to South Africa until the end of the apartheid era.

We have been back a couple of times since, and we are still with David Gresham and his wife Ismay, and the team at their record label. We have always gone down very well in South Africa. It is a beautiful country that has seen tremendous changes for the better in the past two decades. It is a stunning place to visit, and it is wonderful to see how it has changed for the better. And it is nice to be able to return there without becoming the bad boys of the music world.

CHAPTER TWENTY-SEVEN

OLD MICK FOSTER HAD A FARM

MICK

Touring the world was certainly an incredible opportunity. For us two country lads from Ireland, it was beyond our wildest imaginings of what we might achieve when we started out. Tell young Mick Foster that he would be making a living from his accordion by playing around the world and you could have knocked him down with a feather. So we were delighted to get out and about and play our music to the people who loved it.

On the foreign tours we worked for a fee, rather than the door. By working for a fee, we were guaranteed to get paid, and instead the promoter was the one taking a chance. That security was essential to us. It meant when we left Ireland we knew what we would be coming home with. That was important: both of us had families to support. We weren't inclined to take doors, especially in a foreign country where you would not be in control of the promotion. Just like in the pubs of a few years earlier, if a lad is offering you the door, it may mean he is expecting things to go badly. If a lad said I won't give you a fee, but I'll give you the door, you would be better off turning at the door and going home.

For many years now we have brought our own sound engineer with us. That is true no matter where we tour. Seamus Cullinane has been around the world with us. He is also the sound engineer on our albums, so he knows our sound better than anyone. He is able to get the sound in any venue near enough the same as it is on the records, which is a tremendous help. He uses whatever gear is in the venues. All we have to do is turn up and play, which takes a weight off our minds. Given the basic level of the sound checks we had in the early days, we wouldn't be qualified to do more in these bigger venues anyway!

The venues on tour vary in size, from 700-seaters upwards. We have filled 2,500-seat venues but we both prefer the more intimate ones, where you can make a proper connection with the audience.

I have brought my children on tour occasionally – all except the eldest, Jackie. He is a welder and a mechanic now, and he was never bothered with coming away. But the three girls have all been away with me. My oldest, Denise, who is a music teacher, came to Australia and New Zealand with me. And the twins, Sandra and Louise, have been to England, Scotland and Australia. People think that must be fantastic, but the truth is that I am working; I can't just decide to head off and climb Ayers Rock with them. It is nothing like going on a family holiday.

That said, it is great having the company on the road, but I waited until they were old enough to enjoy it. After all, the tour is my work. It's not a holiday. If they were too young it would be pointless bringing them. They would have been bored. But at sixteen they were independent enough to enjoy the experience, and to look after themselves when I was doing a sound check or a media appearance. To them, at least, it was a holiday.

I remember that the tour manager decided to put them to use. He would normally hire someone at the various venues to sell videos and CDs after the performance, but he gave my girls that job. So they were able to earn a right few quid pocket money while they were on holiday!

I would announce at the interval that my twin girls were in the lobby selling the CDs, and during the break people would be all over them. The fans made the girls feel very important, and that went down great with them.

Touring also brought unexpected bonuses, and one of those was the people you meet. We love our fans, and it is great to get a chance to meet them after our shows. We always take the time to come out to the lobby of the theatre or the hotel and sit down for a while, signing autographs and just chatting. It was out of one of these informal sessions after a show in the UK that the Foster and Allen Official International Appreciation Society grew.

It was our spring tour of the UK in 1987, and we were playing in The Victoria Hall in Manley, Staffordshire, on Valentine's Night. Unknown to us a woman sent up a request, but it got lost somewhere and we never read it out. Many people send up requests, especially if it's someone in the audience's birthday or an anniversary, or is battling an illness. We are always glad to read them out. It gives me something to say between the songs!

A month later the same woman was at another of our shows, in the Floral Hall in Southport. This time we did read out her request. She had been ill – that was obvious from what she wrote on the request. I said that we would love to meet her after the autograph session and have a proper chat, if she could stay around.

After the show we were sitting there signing autographs when Pauline Wakefield and her husband Dennis came up and introduced themselves. She was a fierce nice woman, and we both got on with her immediately. She couldn't stay around because she was unwell and in pain, but we were glad we at least got to meet her briefly.

Over the following year there was more contact, and we got to know her a bit. She had been battling health issues for several years, and she credited our music with keeping her sane when the times got tough. Although we were not in the Padre Pio class when it came to miracles, we were delighted our music had been able to help.

In January of the following year, Pauline suggested to us that she found the Foster and Allen Appreciation Society. It's a funny thing when someone asks you something like that. On one level you are chuffed that someone thinks that highly of you. On another level you are thinking, can I supply enough news and help to make this a success? In the end we decided to give it a go.

I'm pleased to say the society is still going strong, even after all these years. Pauline proved to be a great woman, keeping it all on track over the decades. Whenever we are in her part of the UK we try and meet up for a chat or see her after a concert. Over the years we have signed birthday and get well cards for so many people through the society – and the odd sympathy card as well.

There are members in Ireland, the UK, Germany, Canada, Australia – all sorts of far-flung places. Fair play to Pauline. She has done a great job, and we really appreciate it.

By the late eighties success had imposed a rhythm on our year. We would tour in the spring, perhaps to Australia or the UK, then spend the summer at home doing concerts and recording our album for that year. Then we would tour again in the autumn, then have some more time at home. We were crazily busy, but we also had periods in the year when we had time off, and could pursue other interests. And for the first time in my career I had the money to indulge myself.

This led to me almost changing career at the height of Foster and Allen's success! I wanted to get a bit of land as a hobby, but it came close to becoming a full-time job.

To tell the story properly I have to go right back to my childhood. As you know, I was born and raised on a stud farm, and I grew up surrounded by animals. The business of the stud was horses, but I also have fond memories of leading the few Jersey cattle into the yard in the evenings for milking. As a five-year-old, whose head barely rose above the low stone walls, I felt like king of the yard as I led those cattle.

We left the stud, but we didn't leave the country. When my father got his job as chauffeur in Mearescourt House, I was back on a farm again. During the school holidays in my teens I got summer work on the farm on the estate. I would spend the two months farming. I did everything – milking cows, saving hay, thinning turnips – you name it, I did it. It was great to have the few bob in my pocket, but I did it because I loved it.

It was always in the back of my head that I would love to have a bit of land of my own. But it was a number of years before that happened.

Finally, in 1987, I was thirty-nine years old and we were doing well enough that I had the money to go for it. I wanted seven or eight acres, just enough to keep a few horses. I wasn't ambitious. Ten acres was my maximum. I didn't want to be a farmer. I was living in a fine house outside Mullingar with my wife and family, and this would be strictly a hobby.

I had been looking around for a while, and nothing had come on the market. Then a forty-acre farm became available. It was being auctioned in two lots, one of twenty-three acres and one of seventeen acres. The smaller lot was twice what I was looking for, but it was either go for it, or perhaps have to wait for another few years. So I went to the auction.

Unfortunately the Land Commission would not allow the farm to be broken up unless it was sold to existing farmers. As I was new to the game, I had to buy the whole lot. So the non-farmer ended up with forty acres. I had more than four times what I was looking for. That's life, I thought.

When I had that much land I thought I might as well get a few cattle to go with the horses. We had about fifteen suckler cows. A suckler cow is a cow you don't have to milk. I would either use artificial insemination, or bring in a bull, and get the cow in calf. Once the calf was born the cow would rear it until it was weaned. Then we would bring the calf to the cattle sales. The reason I opted for sucklers was that if I was on tour I didn't have to worry about milking a herd twice a day. Sucklers are far less labour intensive, and I was able to run the farm on my own, despite being away a lot.

By the late eighties the rhythm of our year suited my new venture. We were always home for January and February and for most of December. In fact, by 1987 we tended to begin touring after Easter. That allowed me to be home during the winter to look after the animals.

I also kept about twenty-five ewes and three or four horses. The lambing season is spring, and we would sell the lambs to the factory. The earlier the lambs arrived and were ready for the factory, the more they were worth. That suited me: once the lambing was out of the way, I was ready for the road.

Neighbours, and people who were into the horses like myself, would keep an eye on things when I was away. If I planned it right most of the serious work – the lambs and calves – would be out of the way before March.

During the summer I would be home again, for saving the hay, making silage, and all the other farm work. I did all that work myself. A friend of mine, Anthony Darcy, had land just down the road. He was involved in hunting with me – in fact we were joint masters of the Westmeath Harriers. We shared that job, and we shared the farm work. We'd make the hay and silage together. We would cut it and bail it and bring it into his shed and into mine. We are still good friends, and ride out regularly together.

The hobby was now a part-time job, but Foster and Allen were still going just as strong as we ever had. And we were about to receive an invitation to perform at a very special event...

CHAPTER TWENTY-EIGHT

WESTMEATH GETS TO THE ALL-IRELAND FINAL

TONY

From my early days kicking a ball around with my friends, football has been an obsession with me. I played for my school, and all through my life I have followed my parish and my county. Any Sunday that I am not working you will find me at a game. So you can imagine how excited I was in 1988 to be standing in the tunnel at Croke Park, ready to run onto the pitch during the All-Ireland Football Final. And I was playing!

But not football.

Mick and I were there to provide the half-time entertainment at the game, the culmination of the football season. We were joining the Artane Boys Band to add a bit of music to the spectacle. Our appearance sparked a great joke: Who are the only two Westmeath men to have played at midfield in Croke Park during an All-Ireland Final? Foster and Allen.

The most popular sports in Ireland are the two native games: hurling and Gaelic football. Every parish and school has its own team, and the best players also play for their county. Every summer the counties battle it out in the championship, and on the third or fourth Sunday in September the two best counties meet for the All-Ireland football final. It is the most viewed television spectacle in the country, and attracts a huge live audience. There is great pageantry around the game. The Artane Boys Band, a marching band from a school in Dublin, always lead the teams onto the field, and the President of Ireland is a guest at the game.

In 1988 the final was between Cork and Meath, and the stadium was packed. There were 80,000 people on the stands. It was by far the biggest crowd we had ever played before – or ever will again. And the match was shown live on RTÉ, and picked up by Irish clubs and centres around the world. Everyone watches the All-Ireland – we were singing for a television audience of two million. And we had to do it live. This was huge.

Of course, we didn't get seats to watch the match. We were there to work, so we had to watch the action from the tunnels. We were in position fifteen minutes before half-time ended, so we could just run on when the players ran off. We didn't have a great view of the game, but we caught the sense of excitement. It was closely contested, with neither side gaining a clear advantage. Games like that keep everyone on the edge of their seats.

Despite the fact that I am a great football fan, I had not been to too many All-Ireland finals. I am a Westmeath supporter after all. We love our football, but we are not one of the strong counties, and we have never won the championship. But I never missed a final on the television. So like everyone in the country, I was riveted. It was a great place to be on the third Sunday in September, but I had to keep in mind that I was there for the show at half-time, not for the game itself. That was the important thing.

The opportunity came about through Donie Cassidy, who had agreed a deal with Croke Park to provide entertainment at half-time. At the time the GAA were experimenting with bringing a bit more to the half-time entertainment. Traditionally the Artane Boys Band marched the players onto the field at the start of the game, and might strike up a tune at half-time. But with a massive television audience, the GAA decided to make half-time part of the show. A number of artists on Donie's label got the chance over those years, including Declan Nerney, Johnny Carroll and Louise Morrissey. We were delighted to be part of it. To add to the occasion, it was the 100th anniversary of the first All-Ireland Final.

We were asked to do two songs, one for each team. We played the anthem of Cork, 'The Banks of My Own Lovely Lee', and for Meath, 'The Harp That Once Through Tara's Halls', by Thomas Moore. I sang 'The Banks', while Mick sang 'The Harp'. Unlike *Top of the Pops* there was no objection to the accordion, so both songs got the full Foster and Allen treatment.

They brought a small stage out onto the pitch at half-time and placed it right in the centre. We marched rather than ran out – we had to have some breath for the singing. The Artane Boys Band played us on, but when we sang, we sang to a backing track.

I remember we both wore black suits and white shirts. One of us wore a green tie for Meath, and one a red tie for Cork. I can't remember now who wore which, but I suppose I must have been in the red, since I was singing the Banks. It was a good conservative look – there would be no slagging after this performance!

It was a wonderful feeling to be singing in Croke Park before 80,000 people, and must rank as one of the highlights of our career. Throw in the television audience, and I don't suppose it is possible to sing to a bigger crowd. So of course we were nervous. You would be nervous of everything. We were not in control of the sound system – RTÉ, the national television station, was handling that. And there was no rerun if anything went wrong. But in fairness to the people at RTÉ, nothing did go wrong. It all ran very smoothly on the day. We could hear ourselves clearly, which is vital for a singer. So we could relax and enjoy the feeling.

As soon as I opened my mouth, the crowd burst into song with me. I don't think there's a Cork man alive who can't sing 'The Banks'. It was fantastic. The sound swelled through the stadium in a massive musical wave. Imagine tens of thousands of loyal Leesiders belting out their anthem.

It was a huge show to do, and we appreciated and enjoyed every moment of it. All that remains to add is that Cork, despite their wonderful singing, did not manage to overcome the challenge of the Leinster men. The game was a draw, and Cork lost the replay by four points.

CHAPTER TWENTY-NINE

LUCK AND LOSS

MICK

When I first bought the farm we continued to live on the outskirts of Mullingar, and I drove out to do whatever had to be done. But then, sadly, my marriage broke up. I was devastated. That was around 1988.

I have to hold my hands up and admit that it was entirely my own fault. I was never home, and in my earlier days I had a bit of a roving eye. My wife overlooked a few indiscretions, but eventually I got my marching orders. And that was the end of that.

One of the few regrets I have in my life is the break-up of my marriage.

Sheila and I get on well now. In fairness, there never was any hassle. One thing to her credit is that she never used the kids as a lever. I had total access to them whenever I wanted. Three of our children live locally, and so does Sheila, and we get on great. I suppose at the time the break-up was tough on the kids. It certainly was on me. But now we can meet and chat.

So it was bad, but it was not as bad as it could have been.

Once we separated I moved out of the house. It was a terrible time in my life, and I suppose I was looking for a distraction. I decided that I would buy a racehorse. Growing up on a stud, I had the interest. In fact, it was more than an interest: I was delirious to buy a horse. I mentioned it to Tony, and he surprised me. He said we should buy it together. So we did!

We bought the horse at the Derby Sales in Ballsbridge in early 1988 – the last year the sales were held there. My father suggested Francis Flood as a trainer for the animal. He knew Francis, who lived near him. So the horse was based in Grangecon, County Wicklow, under his watchful eye. We called her Nancy Myles, from a song by my friend Kevin Sheerin. Francis Flood Junior was her regular jockey, though she was also ridden by other jockeys, such as Mick Kinane.

Nancy Myles was a good buy. She had her first race in 1989, as a four-year-old, and in her second race, she won. From then on we got used to the winners' enclosure, as she chalked up an impressive list of victories. She won nineteen times in all, including three bumpers, three flat races, three chases and ten hurdles. Three of those hurdle wins were in listed races. She finally retired in 1993.

They named a pub in Tralee Nancy Myles, and we went in there one evening. We asked the man behind the bar where the name came from. He looked at us and said that it was from a horse owned by Foster and Allen. He had no clue he was talking to the same two men!

Mick and I bought a few more horses together, and most of them proved winners, though none was as good as Nancy Myles. Funnily enough, the only horse we had that never won a race was called Foster and Allen. The name was great for us, but it did him no good!

Nineteen eighty-nine, the year Nancy Myles began winning for us, was an eventful year for me. I built a new home on my land. I did most of the work myself, during the months I wasn't on tour. I lived in that house for a number of years, and I had the kids over regularly. It was just as well I had some security around me, because in fact my bad luck wasn't over yet. Nancy Myles might have been winning, but in my personal life more sadness was just around the corner.

When sorrows come they come not single spies, but in battalions. The break-up of any marriage is a matter of great unhappiness, but more tragedy followed. Within a year of my marriage ending, my father passed away.

My da had at least lived to see our success. He saw us on *Top of the Pops*, and he took great pleasure in it all. He was a kind of celebrity himself through Tony and I, at least locally, and he had enjoyed every bit of it. I remember one night we were out together, and Tony and his father were with us. We introduced the two men as Foster and Allen Senior, which went down great! Sadly both men are no longer with us.

My father's death, on 7 July 1989, was an even bigger shock than my mother's had been. He was seventy-three, but in great form. There was no warning. He went out for a couple of pints, came home and went to bed. He was found dead in his bed the following morning. He had died in his sleep. It was a terrible blow to those of us left behind, but if I had the choice of going, that is the way I would pick. When I see people lingering for years and suffering a slow death I think there is a lot to be said for the kick of a horse or an accident. But that is a selfish way of looking at it, because you are thinking of yourself and not the ones left behind.

It was terrible to lose both my parents. You always know it is going to happen some day, but the cold reality takes a lot of getting used to. But there is nothing that can be done, so we must just get on with life.

I have been lucky. I found happiness again with a new partner. And I can thank the music for bringing us together. I have now lived with Moyra Fraser for the past twenty years.

We met as far back as 1983, but I was still married then. It was a number of years before I was free and romance blossomed. We met first when Foster and Allen were touring the UK, hot on the success of 'A Bunch of Thyme' and 'Maggie'. We were still new to the touring business and the big tour coach, and we were enjoying our success.

One of the stops in the tour was in Aberdeen in Scotland. Tony and I went for a bit of a walk, because we had time on our hands. We ended up in a music shop, which I suppose was no great surprise.

There was a lassie there demonstrating accordions and keyboards, and she was very good. It was obvious as soon as we heard her that she had talent. She could almost make the accordion sing, she was that good. We were listening to her for a while, and of course we went over and started chatting with her. We were a bit surprised that she knew who we were, but that was chart success for you. She was Moyra Fraser, and it was no wonder she was so good on the instruments: she was a doctor of music. That put us in our places!

We thought nothing more of the encounter, and we went on with our tour. But over the next few years our tour schedule kept bringing us back to Aberdeen. There is a hotel there, the Douglas Hotel, which is owned by Mary Martin and her partner Robert, who are great friends of Tony's. Mary came from Moate. So any time we were in Aberdeen we would stay at their hotel. We still do.

Mary would throw a small party whenever we would arrive, and she asked Moyra to the parties. So over the years we got to know her quite well, and we were in touch regularly. There was no spark at that stage – I was still married to Sheila.

Sometime after my marriage broke up Moyra came to Ireland to play in a band. She ended up living not far from me. She is a bubbly woman with a great smile and dark chestnut hair. We got friendlier at that stage, and romance began to blossom. We were seeing a lot more of each other, and we both realised that we suited each other perfectly. Over time, we grew very close. More than twenty years ago Moyra moved into my house on the little farm, and made it a home.

Around the same time, Moyra joined Foster and Allen. She is now our band leader. She is talented on so many instruments. She plays keyboards, saxophone and flute, and is great on the accordion. But I say that I have enough competition outside the band as an accordion player without bringing the competition into the band. So she does the keyboards for us. Ollie Kennedy is on bass, and Brian Megahey on guitar, along with Tony.

The structure of the band is this: Tony and I are the bosses. We decide where we are going and what we are doing. But as band leader Moyra is in charge of the music. It is a key role. You need a top-class musician to work out the arrangements and the chords, and we mightn't be good enough to do that. The band leader tells everyone – including us – what to play and when. She is like the conductor of an orchestra. Once the instruments kick in, she is in charge. She arranges the programme and tells us what to do.

She is also a great help to me when it comes to recording. Once Tony and I have decided what we are going to do on an album, we then have to decide how we are going to do it. Tony talks it out with our sound engineer, Seamus Cullinane, who has a great feel for music. I talk it out with Moyra, and she helps me put together the chords and harmonies for my songs. With her background, it is child's play for her.

We work great together. She's a real asset to the Foster and Allen band – and me personally.

CHAPTER THIRTY

THE ROSELAND STUDIO

TONY

If Mick had his interests outside of Foster and Allen, such as the farm, then so did I. With success came the chance to invest in a recording studio in Moate, and I jumped at the opportunity. I loved that aspect of the business, and having our own studio could only help the band. We were recording an album every year, and having our own facilities gave us full control over the process.

It began, as many good things do, almost by accident. By the mid-eighties we were touring extensively, both in Ireland and in England. Dessie and Ollie were on board, and we had a few different people flitting in and out, acting as stage crew. And they did a great job. But we were looking for a permanent sound and light crew, so that would become another aspect of the business we didn't have to think about. If we had our own crew, they would be there and we would know things were just right every night.

One night Seamus Cullinane from Rathdowney in County Laois came along and did our sound. It was my first time meeting him, but we clicked. The minute I met Seamus I said to myself we have to have this man. He was everything we needed. He knew the sound business, he was a great man to work with, nothing was a problem to him, and he would look after everything. That was his nature. He was thorough, but easy to get on with. After the gig I sat down with him and asked him would he be interested in coming on-board and looking after our sound full-time.

He was. He got a van and bought the best of gear, and so we began hiring our sound and light off him. And he has looked after everything from that day to this.

Seamus had a small studio back home in Laois. I had been considering the idea of a studio for a while. I saw an opportunity when I heard that he already had his own. In 1988 I suggested that the two of us go into partnership and open a bigger studio in Moate. He wasn't a man to jump into something without thought. He took a few days, then came back and said that he might be interested. Moate was not far from Rathdowney, so it wasn't like he was relocating to the far end of the country. And he could expand on what he already had.

We talked it out and decided that the old cinema in Moate might be an ideal building. It was no longer being used as a cinema. The upstairs was occupied with a furniture store, a hairdressers, and a solicitor's office. The building was owned by Toss Martin, an old friend of mine and Mick's. I went to Toss and negotiated the purchase of a share in the building. We agreed, and I was half-owner of the old cinema. We took the bottom floor for the new studio.

Seamus was in charge when it came to building the studio and fitting it out. He knew his stuff. He soundproofed the recording area thoroughly, and insulated the whole place. Then he fitted out all the electronics. There was a fair amount of equipment, but he knew it all, and wired it all perfectly. Soon it was ready to go, and we named it the Roseland Studio, after the Roseland

Ballroom, where I had played so often as part of a relief band with the Prairie Boys. From then on Foster and Allen recorded all our albums there, and it became a home away from home for me.

The first album we recorded there was our Christmas Album, released in 1989. It still goes on sale every Christmas. It felt a bit strange singing all the old standards in the middle of the summer, with the sun blazing outside and not a sprig of holly in sight! By that stage our band had expanded. Basil Hendricks was on lead guitar and steel; was there ever a guitarist with a more apt name? We had also added a drummer, Frank Somers, who, along with his wife Mary, had been neighbours of ours in Mount Temple for years. Frank and I travelled together to our Irish gigs for the best part of sixteen years. So it was an awful shock to me when he became ill on one of our English tours, and sadly passed away some time later.

This full line-up gave us a beautiful sound on all the festive favourites I remembered from growing up. We went from the slow and reverential 'Silent Night' to the children's favourite 'Rudolph the Red-Nosed Reindeer', and everything in between. The standards were there – 'Jingle Bells', 'Winter Wonderland', and 'White Christmas' – but we also added a more local flavour with tracks such as 'Christmas Time in Ireland'. We ended with a rousing medley of 'We Wish You a Merry Christmas' and 'Frosty the Snowman'.

It was fun to record, and the album went down very well.

Since that Christmas album we have never recorded anywhere else. We also use the studio as a rehearsal space when planning tours. We get together for three days and work non-stop to get the tour programme just right.

The studio isn't just ours, of course. There is little point in having a studio if only one band uses it. The Roseland was a full commercial studio with the doors open to anyone who had a track they wanted to lay down. Some big names have used the facilities over the years, including Daniel O'Donnell, Brendan Shine, Mick Flavin, Charlie Landsborough, The Whole Shebang and Derek Warfield from The Wolfe Tones. Bob Brolly, a BBC presenter and singer, came over from Coventry to record an album with us. In addition there have been so many local artists – between rock, pop, folk, country and traditional – who have passed through the doors. We were busy.

We were open to everyone, no matter what style they played. A studio is a studio. And ours was a big one, so we could take a full orchestra if they arrived! It was the full size of the bottom of the cinema. The studio itself was a big room with dark sound-damping panels sticking out of the walls at odd angles. It was almost empty, except for the sockets for the microphones, and a few mike stands. Then there was a big glass panel, behind which was the sound-engineer's booth, with the mixing desk and recording equipment. Seamus was the man in charge – when he wasn't on the road with us. Many acts would ask him to engineer their tracks, but as many more brought in their own engineer. Like us they wanted to work with people they knew, and who knew their sound. But it was all good.

The place could be as busy as a railway station. There could be a bunch of musicians and singers warming up, with their musical director putting them through their paces. Seamus would be there as well, keeping an eye on things. In the good times Seamus was there five or six days a week, when he wasn't touring. When he was on the road with us he would have an engineer in there available for recording anyone who needed him. It was a very busy concern.

I was never too active in the business myself. The main reason I got involved is that I wanted Seamus to stay with Foster and Allen. But I also definitely wanted to be involved in a studio. Music was in my blood and I did enjoy immersing myself in every aspect of the process. It was a great experience, but there was never going to be a living for two people in it, so I left the actual running to Seamus.

I always loved being in there, whether I was working or not. As a recording artist there is a great comfort in familiar surroundings. The first time you walk into a studio it can be a daunting place. It is unforgiving. In a gig if you miss a note you play on and the audience stays with you. But if you miss a note in a studio, it is picked up immediately by the producer, and you have to go back and get it right. There is nowhere to hide.

But the Roseland was different. The studio was like home to me. The armchairs had come from my own home. It literally was another living room for me. And psychologically that could only help my performance. The comfort of knowing it is your own studio, and of knowing your own sound engineer/ producer, actually makes you sing better. You are more relaxed, and the notes don't come out strained.

I haunted the Roseland Studio. I loved hanging out there. We had an office in the studio where we handled a lot of the Foster and Allen business. If we were about to tour, a lot of the preplanning was done from there. Flights had to be arranged, venues contacted, and so on. You didn't want to be doing that paperwork from your kitchen table. It was great to have the office. Seamus's wife Mary was the secretary for the studio, and she handled a lot of the office work.

If someone was looking for information on Foster and Allen – maybe a journalist, or a promoter – they could contact the studio and Mary would look after them. When Foster and Allen fans from around the world would call into Moate it gave them a place to visit. They could call on the studio, and they were always assured of a warm welcome. If I was there I could meet them, but if I wasn't, they had something to see at least.

Mary knew our fans better than anyone else and her presence added a homely touch to the whole place, augmenting the friendly atmosphere. She could be dangling her son Adam on her lap, then have to go out to get something, so maybe one of the session musicians or the backing singers would mind him for a few minutes. No one cared; that was the atmosphere in the studio. Their daughter Ciara might be in, doing her homework or running messages. It was family friendly and relaxed. Foster and Allen got completely spoilt, it was so easy-going and laid back. If something wasn't working we could just leave it and come back to it later. Seamus had everything under control. He really became an important part of Foster and Allen, and he still is. You could call him the final member.

In the seventies you would record an album in a day or two. You knew your stuff, and you went in and did it. We were a two-piece, so there was little complication. But not today. Today a lot of planning and preparation goes into a recording, and it is a far bigger job.

In those early days we were assisted by Gordon Smith, and I must digress for a moment, because Gordon was a key part of our success, and became a very close friend of mine. When we were with Ritz Records in the early eighties there was a record company called Ronco. Gordon was with them, and he was the brains behind a very big album called *Green Velvet*, released in 1983. It was a compilation of Irish artists that Ronco brought out after the success of The Fureys, ourselves and Joe Dolan, which they released as a TV album. Ronco was an American television marketing company rather than a record label. They licensed two of our tracks from Ritz Records, 'Maggie' and 'A Bunch of Thyme', for that compilation, which did extraordinary well. It was only released in early December, but still sold 200,000 copies. It was such a success that they followed it with *More Green Velvet* in 1985.

After that the potential of TV albums was obvious. We signed with Tony Naughton at Stylus Records, a company with whom Gordon had become involved. They wanted another album

212

along the lines of *Green Velvet*, which we had featured on. We stuck with Gordon from then to the day he died, moving from Stylus to Telstar when he did, then on to Demon Records. Gordon was involved in all our albums from 1984 to when he died a few years ago.

Gordon was a major part of our success in the UK. He came up with names and ideas for albums and he put together all our TV commercials. All our albums were promoted heavily on television from the moment Gordon got on board – which is probably a big part of why we have had thirty albums in the British charts so far.

Not only that, but he and his wife Paula also became very good friends of ours. From the day I met him to the day he died there wouldn't have been a week that I did not talk to him. If we were not working on an album we would just chat. He was a lovely man, and very interested in the music business. I was very upset when he became ill and within three or four months he was dead.

I have one precious memory of those final few weeks. About three weeks before he died we were working on some new material. He took me aside and asked me to record two songs just for him. The songs were 'In This Life I Was Loved By You', made famous by Colin Raye, and 'The Dance', a big hit for Garth Brooks. They weren't part of the album we were working on. He wanted them for his funeral. 'In This Life' was a tribute to his wife Paula, and it was one of the most moving things I have ever been asked to do.

I had a lump in my throat behind the microphone in the studio, and a tear in my eye three weeks later when the songs were played at his funeral.

Over the years, we have had the pleasure of recording and performing some wonderful songs, and have worked with a wealth of great songwriters. One was Charlie Landsborough, who wrote 'I Will Love You All My Life'. It was through this special song that we first met Charlie and became great friends.

It's hard to think about Charlie without thinking about the Palace Bar in Athlone, owned by Paddy and Eileen McCaul – a place we spent many happy evenings, singing, chatting and just enjoying each other's company, or perhaps listening to Seamus Shannon playing his accordion. Charlie would sing original material, which was unknown at the time. I remember one night after Charlie had finished singing one of his own songs, an old man who was quietly enjoying his pint came up to him and said: 'That was a lovely song you sang there, Charlie, but the next time you write a song, could you write one we know?'

Later on, when I became the proprietor of a small pub in Moate called The Elbow, which was situated directly opposite the Roseland recording studio, Charlie and his wife Thelma would visit the town and soon deemed The Elbow their second home. He quickly became known in The Elbow as the 'hairy man'. He loved the midlands, and I believe the areas surrounding Moate and Mount Temple may even have inspired a few of his songs.

The Elbow only had a six-day license so we were closed on Sundays, which was a bonus for the staff: the manager Pat Claffey, his daughter Sinéad and barmen Damien Campbell and Brendan Grennan – better known as 'Keeshie Babes'. They were all sure of their Sunday off.

There was music in The Elbow on Monday, Wednesday, Thursday and Saturday. Often, musicians from the studio would trip over on their break, or in some circumstances we'd operate a delivery service for some poor soul with a sore throat who just needed a hot port. We also had a pitch and putt club that met on a Saturday morning and headed out rain or shine. As well as this, we had a big punters club, which was a club made up of racing fanatics. The manager Pat Claffey would organise a day at the races for everyone every few months, with a meal on the way home and a session in some other pub. So The Elbow may have been a small pub, but it was a very active one. More importantly, I'm told we served up the best pint of Guinness in the town!

Speaking of songwriters gives me the opportunity to speak of one very close to us – literally – as he has been on stage alongside Mick and myself for most of our career. As Mick says every night when introducing him: 'He has been with us man and boy for thirty years': Ollie Kennedy. Ollie, along with Ber Coleman, wrote a number of wonderful songs for us, including the most requested song we've ever recorded, which I have already mentioned, 'After All These Years'. Ollie: you're some man for one man!

CHAPTER THIRTY-ONE

HELLS ACCORDIONIST

MICK

You wouldn't take me for a biker, but funnily enough I am. I'm no Meatloaf, but I rode high on a Harley for many years. I still love to head off on the bike and amble through the countryside, a knight of the road. But it's a recent development for me. I came at it late in my life, when the success of Foster and Allen opened up the opportunity for me.

Living on the farm allowed me to have my own horses, and my daughters came to love them as much as I did – but not my son Jackie. He preferred motorbikes. The three girls were into horses and hunting and show jumping. It was something we could all do together, and was great fun. But when Sandra, one of the twins, was nine or ten she became allergic to horses. She'd get asthma and every curse of God symptom from handling them. There was nothing we could do; she had to stay away from them. It was a terror, she loved them so much. We'd be out in the fields on the horse, and she'd be stuck inside looking out at us, a long face on her. I felt so sorry for her.

Jackie had been into the motorcycles since he was sixteen, so I had a chat with him about the situation. We decided we'd buy Sandra a scrambler bike so that she could be out in the fields with that. Scramblers were hardy wee bikes, perfect for rough ground, and slow enough that you wouldn't mind putting your daughter on one. Jack went off and resurrected this old bike for her, and got it field-worthy. He taught her how to ride it.

I was looking at all this, and I said you'd better show me how to ride it too. So we both learned, and we had fun on that yoke. I'd never been on one before, but I enjoyed it. It was just the job. She was messing around on it, back in the fields again. And I messed around on it a bit myself.

When she was sixteen I bought her a Honda Rebel 125, which was a bit of a step up. This was a bike you could use on the road, and it was stylish. It looked like a small Harley. I thought I should get something for myself so that I could go out on the road with her. I was horsing around with the others, and I didn't want her to feel left out.

A friend of mine was a Mercedes commercial dealer, and I knew he was a real speed merchant, so he was the man to approach. He had the only Harley racer in the country at that time, and he was a fierce man for the speed. He had a Transit van that could do 160mph. Most of them won't hit a hundred coming down a hill with the wind behind them. This Transit was an amazing machine. You would slide open the back door and there was nothing to be seen but engine. I knew he was my man.

I told him I wanted a bike, and he told me that a Harley Davidson was the only one to go for. He said he would keep an eye out for one. Fair play – he produced a lovely one.

That was my first Harley, and I held on to it a lock of years. I was in my forties by that stage, so I was ready for it. I had fierce manners on the road, because I was old enough to have manners. My father had been a great teacher. Being a chauffeur he had driven for a living, so he knew how to stay alive on the roads. He preached that a motorbike is never dangerous until you get used to it. Before you were used to it you were careful, and it was safe. I always kept that in my head.

Once you have manners on the road, a bike is great fun. I am not a serious biker. I just eejit around on it, having the craic. Speed is not my thing, and I have never really pushed the envelope that way. I did ninety a couple of times. There was a lot more in the bike, but I wasn't bothered about exploring the upper reaches of the speedometer. If you hit a stone at that speed they'd need a brush and shovel to gather you up afterwards.

The first Harley lasted me a good number of years, but eventually I upgraded. I knew more, and of course Foster and Allen was going well, so I had money in my pocket. I was at a Harley rally one time and I saw a guy ride in on a Heritage Softail. It was a beautiful machine and I could see that under me. So I went and bought a new one. It cost €20,000 at that time. I had more money than brains back then. But I had that bike for years. It was a heavy, solid machine that looked amazing.

I don't like light motorbikes, and I don't like light cars. I know they can handle better on a corner and everything, but there is something comforting about a heavy motorbike. I am a fifty miles an hour man rather than a speed merchant, but I still want 1,100cc under me. The Harley had that and more. It had a 1,340cc engine, and growled with power. But it was deceptive. There was a huge windscreen on it that acted like a giant sail, slowing the whole thing down.

I tried it out a few times on private roads, and you wouldn't get 90mph out of it if you kissed its arse. You'd see the needle edging towards 87, 88, but it never went any higher. I pushed it to the limit, but not a hope. Ninety was beyond it.

I held on to the second Harley for a good few years. But then I noticed that I wasn't going out on it as much. The girls were off in college or working or whatever, and there was little motorbiking going on. Maybe once a week in the summer time, and maybe not even that, because it might be raining. We live in Ireland, after all. My expensive bike was at home gathering dust. It was worth too much money for that, so reluctantly I decided my days as a road warrior were over. I sold the Heritage Softail.

Wouldn't you know it, twelve months later I was sorry. I knew I had made a mistake. But I wasn't going to spend that sort of money on a replacement. It had cost a fortune. I was now into my sixties, and I knew I could spend a lot less and get something that would do the job grand. I finally settled on a Yamaha DragStar, which cost me €4,000 second hand. It is not as heavy or as powerful as the Harley. Its engine is half the size. But it is heavy enough, and solid enough. It is a great cruising bike.

Sometimes I will head off with a few musicians who have motorbikes. We'll spend the day touring. Sometimes Sandra and I will relive the old days by heading out on the road. And sometimes I sail off on my own. I will head in whatever direction takes my fancy. I might come to a byroad and wander down to see where it leads. In good weather there is nothing better. I am a fair weather biker. The slightest bit of cold or rain, and I'll stay in. I figure I have a car. I might as well use that if the weather is against me.

Though the bike I have now is lighter and less powerful than the old Harley, she can move a fair bit quicker. I know I could push it well beyond the ninety if I had a mind to. But I'm too old for that sort of messing now. If I hit anything that would be it; I'd be gone. I keep remembering the example of my father. He used to lecture me so much about driving. One of the things he said was that you could come to the brow of a hill, or a bad bend in the road. What if there was a lad there with a drove of sheep or a herd of cattle: are you going to be able to stop? That sank in. To this day when I approach the brow of a hill or a blind corner it pops into my head, and I say to myself to have manners. And I slow down.

Despite this I have managed to pick up four penalty points for speeding. When I travel to Dublin in the car I tend to allow the speed to creep up. It is difficult to avoid on a good motorway. But it could be worse. A friend of mine got six penalty points in the same day. Another got four. He was going to a funeral in Ballinrobe, County Mayo. He got the first two points going up. On his way home that evening he got another two points at the exact same spot! There was a man who wasn't thinking what he was at.

CHAPTER THIRTY-TWO

LIGHTS, CAMERA, ACTION

TONY

By the nineties Foster and Allen had been nearly twenty years on the road. Our early success had been consolidated with sell-out tours all over the world, and our albums continued to do well. We released an album every year, and we were lucky that each one entered the British charts: thirty in a row so far. Our fans have stayed very loyal to us, and we can't thank them enough.

No matter how busy you are touring – and we do tour a good deal – there is a limit to how many people can see you live. Most of our fans buy our music, which is why the yearly albums are so popular – and important.

For decades, music was sold the same way: pressed onto LPs of vinyl. It had been that way from the early days of the twentieth century until almost the eighties – eight decades of LPs and records. Everyone had a gramophone or a record player at home, and that was the standard throughout the world. The only real innovation came in the 1950s when the material the records were pressed onto changed from a mix of shellac and crushed limestone to the lighter and more durable vinyl.

But the last thirty years have seen a whole new range of devices. We have seen tape cassettes, CDs, mini-discs, and downloads. Some, such as the mini-discs, never took off. Others were wildly successful until the next new device came along.

One of the best innovations, at least as far as Foster and Allen was concerned, was the video. Right through the nineties and the early years of the new century videos were a very popular way of selling our music, and we embraced the new format with relish. Not only did it make commercial sense, it was great fun shooting the videos.

The home video cassette recorder was invented in the seventies, and during the eighties took the world by storm. Everyone had a video machine attached to their television, and video shops renting movies sprang up all over the country. Bands quickly began to see an opportunity there, and soon music videos were making an appearance.

In the 1990s and early 2000s, we brought out sixteen videos, all of which did very well. The video would consist of about sixteen tracks, so it was the equivalent of an album. But it had the advantage that the fans could watch you as well as listen to you.

The peak of our success came in 1994. Our video *By Request* stormed up the British video charts. Before we knew it we had reached number three; only Diana Ross and Take That were ahead of us. Both were legends within the business – and that is putting it mildly.

Diana Ross is a musical superstar, whose career stretched from the sixties, with The Supremes, to the present. She has been nominated for an Oscar, won a Tony and a Golden Globe, and been confirmed by the *Guinness Book of Records* as the most successful female artist of all time. Take That were equally impressive. One of the most successful of the early boy bands, they had eleven number-one singles in the UK, and fifty-four worldwide. Their album sales were spectacular; seven number ones in the UK, and thirty-five number ones worldwide. These were no ordinary acts we were competing against. They were musical royalty.

We were thrilled to be sharing the top three spots on the charts with them – thrilled and a little overwhelmed.

A week later we passed Diana Ross, and only Take That were ahead of us. Could we reach the top? It would be huge for us. Funnily enough nobody tracks video sales, so there was no media interest. But it was huge for us and for our record company. This meant an enormous amount, and yet it was a battle that went on almost unnoticed.

I was on tenterhooks all the following week. When the chart finally came out we were thrilled to see we had knocked Take That from the top slot. We were the number one in the video chart. It was a wonderful feeling. It didn't have the public profile of a *Top of the Pops* appearance, but it was in some ways a far bigger achievement. No one sold more videos than us that week – nobody. And videos were huge – they were the most popular format of the day.

We took the videos very seriously. Some bands just recorded concert footage, but we put a lot of thought into our work, and took the entire summer to do them right. The way our year worked then was we would tour in October, November and December, then we were back on the road from March through to the end of May. June, July and August were spent in Ireland shooting the videos for the next release. We would go all over the country shooting, and would do the entire sixteen tracks over those few months. It took a lot of time but it was absolutely great fun.

Our first few videos were shot by TV producer Ian McGarry and talented cameraman Peter Dorney. Later Mick Bracken from Mullingar took over as the man behind the camera. He shot a fierce amount of our videos. We would sit down with him and decide what sort of a video we wanted to shoot. Mick Foster and I had different styles and we sang different sorts of songs. So our videos would be different. We would each discuss with Mick Bracken what we wanted, and do up a storyboard for the shoot. Everything was planned; there was nothing haphazard.

But we couldn't go out and shoot the videos until we had the album of that year recorded. You needed the music to be right before you could begin putting the pictures to it. That was especially true when it came to the singing. The music had to be the same on the video as on the album. Everything had to match, and that took work.

We shot a lot of the videos in various folk parks throughout Ireland. We were lucky to have access to them all. You could find a dozen different farmhouses and farmyards there, old churches, watermills, traditional pubs, and old farm machinery. You didn't have to search hard to find what you were looking for.

I remember shooting the video for 'The Spade'. The plot of the song was simple: Mick was trying to borrow a spade from me, and I couldn't give it to him because he never gave it back to me after the last time he took it. A number like that involved both of us singing, and interacting with each other. To shoot something like that was great fun. At one point Mick tried to follow me into the farmyard and I shut the gate on him, making him climb over it. Some of the videos had a lovely touch of humour to them.

But the more romantic numbers needed a different approach. That is why each one had to be well thought out. We wanted the video to go perfectly with the song. You should have a smile on your face watching the humorous ones, such as 'The Little Shirt Me Mother Made for Me' (with Mick prancing around without his trousers), and maybe a tear in your eye for the sadder ones.

We shot so much gorgeous scenery during those years that Bord Fáilte, the Irish Tourist Board, should have had us on a retainer. On some of the videos we had children singing, and that presented its own opportunity. I come from a very large family, and all of my nephews and nieces have appeared on our videos. I really enjoyed working with them all – I love being an uncle, and hanging out with them. But as the years have passed an unexpected bonus has become apparent, because now I can sit down and look at those videos and see those familiar faces, and the memories come flooding back. I am transported to those happy summers once more. I know that the kids on those videos, adults now, can also look back and see how they were then. They are snapshots of how we used to be. And now those children have children of their own.

Recently my brother Tom shot a video, and he used the children of his nieces in the film. Between his videos and the ones shot by Foster and Allen, whole generations of Allen children have been drawn upon. A talent for singing seems to run in our family, and they all have lovely voices. They are all gifted singers, even if most have not pursued a musical career. Our videos preserve that for posterity. Now as I watch them it is like being transported through the years in a time machine, bringing back all those memories of the Allen children. It is really sweet. They are a legacy of our family.

Family is very important to me, and those memories are a treasure. It was during the height of the video era that my father passed away, in 1993. He had lived to see a lot of the success of Foster and Allen – including seeing two Westmeath men running onto the hallowed turf of Croke Park. I know he had taken great pleasure in it. He had been ill for a while, but he passed away peacefully at home in his own bed, which was a comfort. Looking back the man was a quiet inspiration to me all my life. Several of his qualities that I admired, including his calmness, I hope I have inherited.

Videos continued to be very important to us for a number of years. The video shops used to stack our videos high near the tills, because they sold so well. And if we were on *The Late Late Show* in Ireland, or *The Kelly Show* in Northern Ireland, they would have to make sure that they had an extra large supply on hand. They sold so well they would nearly walk out the door on their own.

Many shops had monitors with music videos playing continuously. Sometimes there would be three monitors at the top of the shop, and three in the back, all showing Foster and Allen! Ours were very popular because of the effort we had put in with the shoots. They weren't concert clips, like a lot of the others. We produced well-thought-out vignettes with each song.

By that time everyone had a video recorder. So it was an ideal way for people to enjoy their music. Records were gradually becoming a thing of the past. Tape cassettes became popular because you could play them in the car or on a Walkman. Later CDs became popular for the same reason, making vinyl obsolete. So when people came to replace their record players, many opted for the new video machines. We gave people the choice – they could listen to us on cassette, on LP, or on video. One of the great advantages of video was that it didn't scratch like vinyl and it tended to remain in good condition far longer. And they made a great gift. If it was coming up to Christmas and a young lad wanted to get something for his granny or an uncle, he could pick up a video for a tenner, wrap it up and the job was done.

For all these reasons over a few short years the videos completely wiped out LPs. By the mid-nineties when a record shop was ordering our music they might buy a hundred copies on cassette, fifty on CD – and a hundred and fifty on video. That is how important they were. Our videos such as *Souvenirs and Memories, Heartstrings* and *By Request* were great successes.

And then, as quickly as it begun, the era of the videos was over. DVDs replaced the video cassette recorders. Now, only a decade and a half after its glory days, video is almost obsolete.

You would struggle to find a video player today, and the video shops have all switched to the new formats – or disappeared. You would think it would not make a huge difference, but it has. For some reason people don't purchase music on DVD the same way they used to on video. But we are seeing some signs that that is beginning to change again. A new generation of country musicians and singer/songwriters are reviving the format.

So today our year has changed; we no longer have to take the summer months off to traipse around Ireland looking for locations. But last year we spent two months in the summer recording our own television series *The Foster and Allen Show*, for Sky. So perhaps things haven't changed all that much after all.

In addition to the videos, the other way our fans got to see us was through television appearances. For a while we were doing *The Late Late Show*, the biggest chat show in Ireland, nearly every year. *The Late Late Show* is the longest-running chat show in the world – and still going strong. For decades it was presented by Gay Byrne, before Pat Kenny took over. Now Ryan Tubridy is in the presenter's seat, and doing a great job. In its heyday it could make a career. Our first appearance was when 'A Bunch of Thyme' hit number one in Ireland for the first time, in 1979. We were still a single-channel country and that made us a household name. I loved Gay Byrne – he was so easy to work with.

Most of our appearances were as musicians. We would come on, sing our song, and disappear. But occasionally he would interview us as well. He was always well prepared, and the interviews were enjoyable. Once Gay retired Pat Kenny took the show in a slightly different direction, featuring more current affairs. We were never on during his time, but now Ryan Tubridy has gone back to the light-entertainment format, and we have appeared a number of times. I like Ryan Tubridy, and I think he is very good at his job. It is a tough job, and he is a fierce nice fellow. We were delighted to appear with him.

Over the years we did so many shows, with so many different presenters. We did *Live at Three* with Thelma Mansfield and Derek Davis. This was Ireland's most successful daytime television programme, and ran for more than a decade, reaching audiences of 300,000. We also did *SBB ina Shui*, with Sean Bán Breathnach, an Irish language light-entertainment show with a great touch of humour. BiBi Baskin featured us a number of times on her show, as did Liam Ó Murchú on *Trom agus Éadrom*, and Doncha O'Dualaing, as well as TV3's *Breakfast Show* with Mark Cagney and company. One time, we even appeared on a show presented by former world featherweight boxing champion Barry McGuigan. We found them all great to work with.

Gerry Kelly in BBC Northern Ireland was good to us as well. He had the most popular chat show in the province, going out every Friday night. North of the border he was as important as Gay Byrne was south of the border. And both Eamonn Holmes and Gloria Hunniford began their successful careers on Northern Irish television. They were equally supportive of us. In the UK we did *Pebble Mill At One*, *This Morning*, and a number of afternoon chat shows.

When you got an appearance on *The Late Late Show* or on *The Kelly Show* it was meant to remain a secret until the evening of the broadcast. But it was important for the record companies to make sure our CDs, LPs and videos were in plentiful supply in the shops for the following day. If you didn't have loads of records in the shops, you were in trouble. They would fly off the shelves in huge numbers. Those television shows were a very big deal to us.

If we had a gig on Saturday (or Friday with Kelly) we would just have to try and work it all out. Most venues in Ireland were very sound when it came to clashes like that. They knew how important it was, so they would let us change the date, or maybe swap with another act. Occasionally we would have to cancel, but mostly we could postpone or just move the date. Around the time 'A Bunch of Thyme' and 'Maggie' came out we were still touring the lounge bars and cabaret venues around the country, and often gigging five, six or seven nights a week. We would be playing the same venue maybe five or six times a year, and the television appearance was as important to them as it was to us – they wanted a full venue. The television exposure helped that. So they would be as accommodating as they could be.

On a Friday when we had a television appearance to do we would clear the whole day. It wasn't just a matter of showing up on the night and doing our piece. We would have to go in early to do the sound check and rehearsal in the studio. The rehearsal wasn't for us; it was for the cameraman so he could get the right shots. It was also a technical rehearsal, to get the band or the backing tracks sounding right. We had our act rehearsed to the last, so it wasn't for our benefit. We had it well polished always.

The technical rehearsal could last a half an hour or more. And we'd be delighted if it took that length. There were no complaints from us: we knew that the more times we went through it the better it would get. It would look and sound great on the night. We might go through the entire song four times, with a break between each one so that they could adjust their cameras and lights. Then we were done. They would tell us to come back at eight for make-up.

Depending on when we were finished we might kill the intervening time by heading off to the canteen, or lying down for a while and relaxing. Then it was into make-up, which never took too long. They were very professional. A dab of powder so that we didn't shine under the lights, and a bit of tidying up, and we were ready. Then we would wait in the green room (avoiding the hospitality!) until someone came and led us quietly into the studio, where we would be ready to make our entrance.

It was a strange feeling waiting in the wings. We would be surrounded by wires and cables, in semi-darkness. But ahead of us were the set and the bright lights. I didn't think I was that nervous before a television performance, but I have learned to recognise a few symptoms of nervousness in myself. In me it comes out as a pain in my stomach. Before every appearance on *The Late Late Show* I felt that pain in my stomach. That will tell you how important it was to us.

There is something special about *The Late Late* that other shows don't have. So many acts have built their careers on the strength of a good performance on that show – and not just musicians. Comedians such as Tommy Tiernan and Brendan O'Carroll, and writers like Alice Taylor, have all benefited from the special magic.

Those appearances were a big deal for us, and they translated into record sales – so they were a big deal for the record company! Now that we are a concert act we are not on the road every night of the year, so it is a lot easier to fit in the television appearances around our schedule. But they are as important as ever, and we are grateful to every show that ever had us on.

In more recent times a new generation of presenters have been equally good to us – though the style of the shows have changed a lot! We still do *The Late Late Show* with Ryan Tubridy on occasion, but we have also done some shows that would never have gone out in the old days.

Two that stand out are *The Tommy and Hector Show* on regional radio, and *Podge and Rodge*, on RTÉ television.

The Tommy and Hector Show is presented by comedian Tommy Tiernan and television personality Hector Ó hEochagáin. Both are natives of Navan who have built up huge followings. Tommy is one of the funniest – and most controversial – comedians in the country, while Hector has revitalised Irish-language broadcasting with his antics.

We ran into Hector in Australia of all places. He was out there recording one of his television shows, which involved him travelling all over the world. We were touring. He met us at a venue called Rooty Hill, outside Sydney. He came in and recorded a number with us on the night, which went out on his TV show. We got on with him great.

At home Hector teamed up with Tommy Tiernan on a new radio station. i102-104 was based in Galway, and broadcast to seven counties in the west and north-west, and was aimed firmly at a youth audience. They also had a studio in Athlone. They were not our crowd – you don't see too many twenty-year-olds at a Foster and Allen gig. But when they invited us onto the show, we were delighted to go along.

We had fierce craic with the two lads for an hour one morning. It was hilarious – completely over the top, but it opened us up to an entirely new audience. And that is never any harm. I love those kinds of shows, because they are so different.

The other show that stands out in recent years was *A Scare at Bedtime*, with Podge and Rodge. Podge and Rodge are two puppets. They are middle-aged farmers who inhabit Ballydung Manor somewhere in the midlands. They have a savage sense of humour and they take no prisoners. Though it is a puppet show, you wouldn't let your kids watch it. It is aimed firmly at a more mature audience.

The show went out once a week, late at night, and quite quickly they introduced two great characters – singing farmers Fester and Ailin. They were quite clearly a parody of Mick and me, and they were hilarious. Their song titles tell you everything you need to know – 'Doing the Wife's Sister', 'Never Shove a Banger up your Arse at Halloween', 'Tropical Diseases', and 'Never Turn your Back on a Monkey'.

They claimed that Mick and I had stolen their act, and we had also stolen their hit, 'A Bunch of Lesbians', and changed the words! You know you have it made when you are parodied like that. It is the equivalent of an English act being on *Spitting Image*.

The programme was a great success, and Podge and Rodge got their own Christmas special. We were invited to come on. We were able to defend ourselves against the charge of stealing their act. A number of celebrities were on discussing their favourite Fester and Ailin songs. It was all great fun. We also re-aired the whole controversy over 'Bunch of Thyme' and 'Bunch of Lesbians'.

Normal run-of-the-mill shows are great, but when you appear on something like *Podge and Rodge* it broadens your horizons. It opens you up to an entirely new audience. People that would never have thought about us were watching us on the television. And some of them might like what they saw, and check us out.

Podge and Rodge made us cool. You can't complain about that!

CHAPTER THIRTY-THREE

HORSES, HOUNDS AND HOUSES

MICK

By 2004, my so-called 'hobby' farming the land was starting to become a job in itself, and, of course, I was getting older. I had become a farmer by accident, and it didn't take too many years before I realised I had taken on more than I should have with the forty acres. In 2004 I took a big step: I sold the house, stables, outhouse and most of the land. I got rid of it all, keeping only seven and a half acres. That was what I had wanted in the beginning. I built another new house from scratch on the small parcel of land, and that is where Moyra and I live to this day.

The house I built was an Austrian house. It was designed by an Austrian company working with Caoilte, the Irish forestry body. Based on a traditional Austrian design, it is eco-friendly, and built from timber. It is a comfortable three-bedroom dormer house, and we bought it turn-key. We didn't have to do a thing. It was painted and tiled, and the timber floors were down. The kitchen was fitted. All we had to do was bring in the bed and go to sleep.

It was expensive, but it was perfect for me. I haven't got the time any more to be messing around on a building site. I have built a few houses for myself over the years, and that was grand when I had the time. But when you don't that sort of messing is no fun.

As well as the house I built an American barn. We all know the Irish barns – a big old shed with a galvanised roof and one or two of the sides open. The American barn is a more substantial structure. It has got 2,000 square feet of floor space, and inside it are three boxes that I use as stables. I also have a tack room. The rest is open space. I can store firewood, put two or three cars in there, store feed and bedding for the horses, and anything else I want. My motorbike is in there, push bikes, everything.

The reason I only have the three loose boxes for stabling is that if I had more, I might be tempted to have more horses! Now I can have only three. At one stage I had eleven horses in addition to the cattle and ewes, and the hobby became a job. I am not going back to those days; it was too much work.

I have just three horses now, and not a thing else. My grandson Daniel keeps his thoroughbred there. He is a talented amateur jockey, and rides points-to-points all over the country. I also have a three-year-old draught horse. I bought him as a yearling, and I broke him. Daniel got him jumping. We will probably sell him at the back end of this year.

The final horse is my hunter. He is eighteen years old now, so I have been riding him almost two decades. We still go out regularly.

Funnily enough I didn't ride all my life. Growing up on a stud, and later at Mearescourt Estate, I used to jump on the back of donkeys and asses and farm horses like any young lad. But I never learned to ride properly. And some of those animals ran away on me, and threw me badly. They frightened the life out of me. So when I reached adulthood I was terrified of getting onto a horse. I was happy to watch them from the crowd.

Then, in the early nineties, Tony and I went on an entertainers' day out with a bunch of other lads in the business. I can't recall everyone who was there that day, but I remember some of the Bards were with us, and Dublin comedians Paul Malone and Brendan O'Carroll (of *Mrs Brown's Boys* fame). There were about twenty-five of us altogether. We began the day with a round of golf, then we went to a place that had all sorts of activities such as archery, clay pigeon shooting and riding. As soon as we got to the riding ring twenty-four of us jumped onto the back of horses and were soon trotting around the ring happily, tackling little six-inch jumps and feeling like kings. And I was at the fence. There was no way I was going to ride.

You can imagine the slagging I got – twenty-four colleagues, all flapping their arms and making chicken noises. I said to myself, by Jesus the next time I go on one of these trips, I will be able to ride.

I approached a friend of mine who was a racehorse trainer, and I asked him to find a riding instructor who would teach adults how to ride. He put me in touch with Anthea Rainsbury, who was based near Mullingar. I went to her, and I learned the basics. I learned how to sit properly in the saddle, how to trot, canter and gallop, then how to take jumps. And I found I loved it. She started me off, and it went from there.

I had a bit of land by that stage, and a few horses. I was finally able to ride on them. I joined the Westmeath Harriers, the local hunt. Most counties have a local hunt, and a pack of dogs. Westmeath, for reasons unknown to us all, has five local hunts. There is the Westmeath Foxhounds and the Westmeath Harriers, my crowd. In theory the foxhounds go after foxes, and we should chase the hares. In reality nothing gets killed, because that is not the purpose of the day. Then there is the Streamstown Harriers and the South-West Meath Harriers, and the Glasson Farmers, based out near where Tony came from.

That's five packs, which curtails the ground we can cover quite a bit.

Not everyone welcomes a pack of hounds and a horde of horses trampling over their land. But luckily many of us are landowners, and we have enough space for the job. There are seven or eight jumps on my land, and the lad beside me has fourteen jumps around his. Within a fifteen-mile radius there are plenty of places we can go. It is an extended cross-country run. We gallop, we jump fences and ditches, and we have great craic altogether. But we never kill anything.

The hunting season starts on the first Sunday of November and ends on the last Sunday of February – which suited my touring schedule. I threw myself into it with a passion when I was home. What a wonderful way of spending a Sunday afternoon. I got involved in organising things too, and for ten years I was joint master of the hunt, with my friend Anthony Darcy. But that is in the past. Now I just ride out when I get the chance.

I also ride out in the summer for the pleasure of it. I might go up and down the road, or I might head to the lake, which is only two miles away. Sometimes a few of us will ride to the lake and let the horses splash around in the water, more for relaxation than anything else. It is total fun.

I don't go out hunting every Sunday any more. If Daniel is riding in a point-to-point within motorcyling distance I will fire up the motorbike and go and support him. But I still enjoy it. However, things have changed. For one thing, at my age you no longer bounce. It is no fun getting thrown any more. You don't shrug it off, it can hurt, and it can take a few days for the aches and pains to go. For another thing, many of the people I used to ride out with have retired. Now I am the oldest member of the hunt.

On a Sunday a new generation will be coming up to me and saying, 'How's it going, Mick?' And Mick won't have a clue who they are. There was a time I had to ask someone who his father and mother were to know who he was. Now I have to ask him who his grandfather and grandmother were! It's a sign of age. I still enjoy it, but I don't have the same craic and fun I used to.

My horse is eighteen now. When he decides he has had enough, both of us will bow out gracefully. I definitely won't be going out with another horse. The day will come when the horse or myself decides we have had enough, and that will be our joint retirement. But I will look back with great pleasure on those years with the Westmeath Harriers.

It is funny how I have mellowed as I have grown older. There was a time when nothing mattered to me beyond the music. I still love it – I still play impromptu sessions with friends, and travel to fleadhs when I am not on the road with Tony. I still love being in the studio recording new tracks, and being in front of an audience and entertaining them. But as the years have passed I have broadened my interests. I am lucky that Foster and Allen has allowed me to have a great life.

CHAPTER THIRTY-FOUR

NEW JOY AND SAD TEARS

TONY

It was through music – and the recording studio I had set up with Seamus Cullinane – that I met my wife, Trionagh. We have been together twelve years now.

I remember the day well. It was back in 2001, on 10 May, and we were recording the album *Sincerely*. You always need backing singers on an album, and one of our regulars was not doing it any more. So Kevin Sheerin, my old pal from the Kieran Kelly Band days, who was producing that album, had suggested that Trionagh would be a great replacement. He also wanted two lads with her on the harmonies. He asked me to come in to the studio and listen to the three. I was glad to; it was my second home at that stage.

As soon as I saw her I remembered we had met before, on a tour of America where she was working with Dominic Kirwan. I am a naturally shy man, and I don't think I had made a huge impression on her in America. But we got on famously that day in the studio, and at the end of the recording session I surprised myself by asking her for her phone number. I was not looking for love, but it had snuck up on me. I felt an instant attraction to her. We have been inseparable ever since.

Trionagh had owned a record shop where we sold in huge numbers, so I was well in there! She was also a backing singer with Daniel O'Donnell, and an independent session musician. She had sung on albums by Brian Kennedy, Dominic Kirwan, Van Morrison and Charlie Landsborough, and also recorded her own country album.

For the next few years we lived together on and off. By on and off I don't mean there was any lack of commitment in the relationship. Far from it. But she lived in the North at the time. When we met, her youngest, John, was still in primary school. My children were older, but I was still in Moate, where they were. My marriage had broken up a number of years previously. And Trionagh was often on the road with Daniel O'Donnell, while I had to tour with Foster and Allen. As all our children grew up, it became easier to be together all the time, which has been a delight.

In 2009 we got married. Trionagh came off a tour with Daniel on 30 August – and on the last night they threw a party for her, so she was exhausted! On 3 September we walked up the aisle. It was a beautiful ceremony and we involved all the family. My son Ian's wife, Sutanya, was Trionagh's bridesmaid, and my other son Keith was my best man. It was lovely – all the children were at the wedding, Trionagh's and mine.

Ours is not a normal marriage, in that we are away a lot. But absence makes the heart grow fonder. When we come back from tour we have such a lot to talk about. I live in Lurgan now and I love my life there. We live a quiet life, enjoying the comforts of home after weeks on the road. We might go out for a meal or a drive and we are often accompanied by Trionagh's mother, Gertie, who is a wonderful woman and great company.

I think it is healthy to work separately. We are both musicians, who enjoy the same things. And we love each other's children.

Trionagh has two sons. Lee, aged thirty, has a law degree and has moved to Australia for a while. John is nineteen and studying his Bachelor of Music degree at Queen's University in Belfast.

We met through music and stay together through music. It is a recipe for happiness.

I wish that all of life could be that happy – but everyone is visited with their fair share of tragedy as well. In 2004 I was devastated when my sister Mary passed away. She was the first of us to go, and it hit us all hard.

Three years later, in early 2007, Maisie, my brother Mick's wife, sadly died. She was a lovely woman, and a dynamo of energy who was involved in everything in the community. She had a tremendous interest in young people, and not just her own brood. The underage football teams, the swimming club, they all benefited from her energy and input. Her funeral was one of the biggest I can remember – there were hundreds of cars in the car park and even more mourners. This caring woman had touched so many lives.

Mick's health went into a decline after Maisie's death, and he passed away two years later. I still miss him.

But fate hadn't finished with us yet, and tragedy struck that family a third time a few years later, when their son David died of a brain tumour. If there is any comfort for us as a family, it is that they are all together now in heaven. David is so sadly missed by his wife Tara and their two beautiful children, Kayleigh and Shaney, and by his brothers Michael, Kevin, Jimmy and Philip, and sister Moira. It was a hard thing to experience, but there was nothing any of us could do but celebrate their lives and try to move on with our own.

CHAPTER THIRTY-FIVE

TROUBLED TIMES

MICK

As the years stretched into decades Foster and Allen went from strength to strength. We toured, we made records, we sold out concert venues. And we believed we were paying our taxes.

Unless you were living in a ditch the past number of years it would be difficult not to know that Tony and I have had problems with the Revenue Commissioners over our tax affairs. And it came as much of a surprise to us as it did to our fans.

As the matter is still before the courts I cannot say much. By rights I should not say anything. But I will say this: I never set out to do anything underhand, and I was as shocked as anyone when I discovered the problem. As far as we were concerned we were compliant, but the issue arose because we had a bad advisor looking after our affairs.

We had hired an advisor, Patrick Russell, to help us. It turned out that was a big mistake. I cannot say much, but Russell, a qualified barrister and accountant, has since been struck off as a barrister for professional misconduct (unrelated to our woes). We picked the wrong man.

As long as I live I will never forget the day I heard the news for the first time. It was the spring of 2008, and we were touring in the UK. I was relaxing in the tour bus, heading down the motorway, when my phone rang. It was early in the day – we weren't long on the road. I answered the phone and got the shock of my life.

'You are up before the court in Mullingar in an hour, and if you don't have someone there to represent you the court will issue a warrant for you,' I was told.

If I hadn't been sitting down you could have knocked me over with a feather. The colour drained from my face. I had no idea what it was about. It was like the ground had suddenly opened up beneath me. I was floored. I'd thought everything was in order.

It turned out to be far worse than either of us could have imagined. Revenue said that we both owed close to a million each. And they were adding fines and penalties on top of that. My first thought was that we are not U2. We have done very well, but we are not in that league! There has been one High Court case already, and there is a Supreme Court Appeal pending. But we hope the day will come when we can put this behind us.

Tony and I are doing all in our power to get our affairs back in order.

Sad to say, other troubles followed our tax woes.

As the decade drew to a close, I lost my dear sister Patricia. She was eleven days after of her forty-ninth birthday, but she had been battling cancer for some time. The cancer went away, but then it came back again. It was a rare form, and the doctors were honest with her from the beginning. She knew what she was facing, and she faced it with tremendous dignity and a great sense of humour.

She used to joke that she would be the healthiest-looking corpse ever, and it was true: she never looked sick a day of her life, even nearing the end.

I admired the courage and humour she showed. She was upbeat all the time. It is only when these people are gone from your life that you realise what a tremendous hole they leave.

We were a small family, and I am the only one left now.

But that is life. I have a wonderful partner, four beautiful children, and audiences to share my music with. Taken all in all, I have led a charmed life. And I know it.

CHAPTER THIRTY-SIX

THE SKY'S THE LIMIT

TONY

I would very much like to explain to our fans the exact circumstances of our tax problems. However, due to the legal situation and the ongoing nature of the issues, my hands are tied on this and I can unfortunately say no more at this time without compromising the situation.

But life has to go on. With no alternative – and in part to try to take my mind off the enormity of what was going on – I threw myself into what I loved most: my music. I entered the recording studio with my sleeves rolled up and I tried to focus on the latest album we were making that year.

We do an album every year, which is a great constant to me, especially in such difficult times. They are usually a lot of fun to prepare for. The Roseland Studio, my home away from home, was always where we did our work. The studio had brought Trionagh and I together, and it was also the scene for many happy times in my professional life too. Mick and I still spent a couple of months every year in there, getting that year's album ready. November is a good time to release an album, at least for us. It comes out in plenty of time for the Christmas market, and people can buy it as a gift. It makes commercial sense for it to come out then. But the work starts a lot earlier than then. In fact we start planning an album before Christmas the previous year! A full year goes into doing it right.

We begin by having a meeting with Donie Cassidy and his son Peter in CMR Records in Dublin. Then we might fly over to London to meet with the people in Demon Records, who look after our record sales in the UK. The lads in London might say that they feel an album of sixties music would do well at the moment, so Mick and I would begin researching songs from the sixties that would suit Foster and Allen. That is not as easy as it sounds. You don't just pick the twenty songs you like to listen to. They might not suit the configuration of the band, or our singing styles. They have to be songs we are drawn to, but that suit us as well.

The lads at Demon Records, Michael Niedus and Adrian Sear, might come up with a list of songs too, and we will come up with our own list. Donie might throw in a suggestion. Then we will narrow those lists down to the tracks we are going to record. There is no point going into a studio unless you know what you are going to be doing in there. Once we have our twenty songs, we then decide which are Mick's and which are mine, and what we will be doing on each one. I will take my list and chat with Seamus. Mick takes his list to Moyra Fraser, his partner and the musical director of our band. She produces his numbers, while Seamus and I produce mine. We have to decide what key the songs will be in, what instrumentation will be behind them, and what order we will lay down the tracks.

Generally we will lay down the drums, piano, bass and maybe acoustic guitar. Mick will play the accordion at this stage, and I will do whatever playing I need to do. Then we do a guide vocal – but it won't be the final vocal. Laying down each layer might take a day or two. But if it does, they won't be just doing one song. They could lay down the drums for six songs today, then lay down the bass for those six tomorrow. That is how it works, building up the sound layer by layer.

Once we have the guide vocal in place we are ready to begin filling out the final sounds. The guide vocal is needed to help the musicians who are doing the strings and steels and leads. Once their contribution is in place Mick or I come in and do our few days on the lead vocals. At that stage we bring in the backing singers and lay down the harmonies.

It's a complex process. You could put down eight tracks in a day or two, then work on the next layer. You might have acoustic guitar in one day, but you won't have the lead guitar in the same day. It is four to six weeks of constant work. In the old days we came together as a group and played the music, which the sound engineer recorded. Now we each do our bits separately, and they are combined later. You get used to it, but until you hear the final sound, it doesn't feel like a piece of music.

Of course there are some tracks that just don't work, even after all the work, and occasionally a track is dropped during the recording process.

But the job isn't over yet. Now the layers have to be mixed by the engineer/producer to get the right final sound. He might go through three mixes before he and I are happy we have nailed it. It is labour intensive. Seamus absolutely loves his work, and he is musical. To him it is a labour of love. I know it is a job, but it is more than a job in that sense. He is a bit of a perfectionist. If you are the one in the studio behind the microphone you might be inclined to say something is good enough; it will do. But if Seamus is not happy, he'll say: Not yet – it's not sounding the way it should. Try again.

In the end we all want to get it right.

From the beginning we have been committed recording artists. We have released an album every year, and those albums have done very well, both at home and abroad. The backbone of that achievement has been the Roseland Studio. But unfortunately the old Roseland is no more.

I will never forget that horrible night. It was a Tuesday, 27 October 2009, and I was at home in Lurgan and fast asleep when I got the call. Groggily I got up from bed and answered the phone. It was my son Ian. He still lives in Moate. He told me that there was smoke coming out of the door of the studio. At that stage he could not see where the smoke was coming from, or how bad the situation was. He just phoned the fire brigade and phoned me.

I turned to Trionagh and said there was a problem in the studio and I needed to get there as quick as I could. I got dressed and got into the car, driving through the night in a terrible state, wondering what I would find when I got there. Of course I knew there was nothing I could do. I would be just picking up the pieces. But I had to see for myself what the damage was.

It turned out the fire had broken out upstairs, not in our studio. But of course the fire spread. By the time I arrived there were massive flames shooting out of the building. The roof was gone and the structure of the building was destroyed. Because of the layers of insulation and soundproofing the studio was not as badly damaged as upstairs. But it was still destroyed. When the embers cooled down and we were allowed to enter we were able to save a few bits – the sound desk and a few other things. But we lost a lot to smoke damage, heat, and water damage from the fire-fighting efforts.

The Roseland Studio was no more. I knew it as I looked at the smouldering building. I was right; a few weeks later the entire building was torn down. It was terrible to see it in ruins. I was terribly upset, but no one had been hurt, and that was all that mattered. So much of our lives were tied up in the studio, but we would soldier on. It was only stuff; stuff can be replaced.

But, phoenix-like, the Roseland rose from the ashes. Seamus got a new building in Moate and he rebuilt the entire operation, keeping the Roseland name. Fair play to him, he was back in business in short order. But this time I was not involved. It is Seamus's studio now. I don't have my armchairs there, and I am not there myself, unless work brings me. For one thing I live in County Armagh now, a number of hours' drive away. So in that sense there has been a massive change.

But in another sense things are the same as ever. When we do go to record, we enjoy the same friendly atmosphere, and the same banter. Seamus is still Seamus, and it is a great comfort to know that our own sound engineer, a man who has been through it all with us for so many years, is still behind the desk. I know our albums are all the better for that.

Whatever life throws at you, you have to pick yourself up and keep doing what you do. Foster and Allen are no different from anyone else in that respect. We continue touring and continue recording. In the last year, we have got a chance to dig out all the old videos we shot during the nineties, and put them to use. We were delighted to be commissioned for our own television series on Sky TV, and we were able to share the videos with our fans all over again.

Sky TV channel 191 is called *Showcase*. It might not be the most high-profile channel in the Sky stable, but it can be seen all across Europe, and it features a number of Irish music programmes, such as *Hot Country*, *Ireland West*, *Top Country*, *The Phil Mack Show* and many more. Our tracks would have been played on many of those shows. It is the sort of channel that people who are into our sort of music tend to tune into.

Peter and Donie Cassidy saw the opportunity, and they negotiated our own show on the channel. We had a stockpile of videos we had shot in the nineties, and it would be a great way of showing them all again. They thought it would be a great promotional tool for us, as well as providing an entertaining show for our fans.

In the past we might have spent the summer travelling the highways and byways of Ireland looking for locations for those videos. Now we only had one location to worry about – the studio from which to present our show. In 2012 we spent the summer in the studio recording our thirteen-part series. It was a lot more relaxed than the old filming days, but in its own way every bit as rewarding.

We chose familiar ground for the studio; we recorded the series in Seamus's rebuilt Roseland Studio. We were at home there, and it was the perfect location. Our old director Mick Bracken was back on board: he brought in the cameras and shot the entire series for us. Caroline Cunningham – who has made us look good on our videos so many times – came in to put a bit of powder on us, and took years off us. It was quite an easy show for us to do. The backbone of the show was the videos. And as we had released sixteen videos, and each one featured fifteen or sixteen tracks, we were spoilt for choice.

On familiar ground, we were able to relax. We sat on two chairs in the studio, Mick with his accordion and me with the guitar, and we introduced each video, and shared our memories of the stories behind each one. We'd talk about the people in the videos as well. Watching those videos brought back some great memories for both of us.

And the programme wasn't all Foster and Allen. We featured a few other artists, for variety. It was important to us that the show would appeal to everyone, and the guest artists added to the interest. We even interviewed some of them live, including Terry Wogan! Terry, from Limerick, had emigrated to the UK and became the most popular chat show host on the BBC, as well as being that country's top radio presenter. He was a great champion of our music, and one of the key factors in our early success. When he began playing 'A Bunch of Thyme' and

'Maggie', the regional BBC stations followed suit, and soon we were climbing the charts. It was a great honour to have him on our show. We were delighted to meet with him again.

The filming was hectic. Under Mick Bracken's direction we shot two shows a day. Then he got on with the editing, which took another few weeks. *The Foster and Allen Show* was a truly Westmeath production. The editing and post-production work was all carried out by Mick Bracken Productions, and Niall McGowan of NRG TV Productions. Both are based in Mullingar. When it was ready to roll we were helped by Seamus O'Connor, who has handled our UK publicity for years. He has been a loyal friend, and has been instrumental in organising a lot of our video and TV appearances in the UK, including this one.

The programme was first broadcast on Monday 24 September 2012. It went out early, from seven to eight o'clock. Viewers all over Ireland, England and Europe – wherever Sky was available – were able to watch. And the shows got a huge response.

The variety helped – it wasn't just a succession of our videos. That first show featured the late Joe Dolan. Other weeks we featured Daniel O'Donnell and the Irish Rovers, as well as ourselves. Daniel was no stranger to our studio; he had recorded an album at the Roseland. During the first show we had footage from a special *Gay Byrne Radio Show*, never before broadcast. We went to an effort to give value. If people were going to sit down for an hour, we tried to make that hour as entertaining as possible.

When you do something like our television show you are not quite sure how it will go down until the feedback comes in from the fans. The programme went out from September to November, and during that time we did a tour of England. Our fans quickly let us know they had enjoyed the series.

Because the programme was so well received other channels showed an interest, and TG4, the Irish-language station, bought the series. It began airing on that channel in the summer of 2013. The timing could not have been better – the series was halfway through when we returned from Australia and our summer tour of Ireland began.

Having our own television show was great; it gave us full control of the production. However we were no strangers to the small screen, after three decades or more on the road. Television has been great to us, and, who knows? Maybe we might do more of our own shows in the years to come.

INTO THE FUTURE

MICK AND TONY

Foster and Allen have been on the road thirty-eight years now, and they have been thirty-eight wonderful years. In some ways concert musicians lead privileged lives. We travel the world, bringing our music to people who are delighted to hear us. If you enjoy what you do you will never work a day in your life.

Looking back, there have been so many highlights. Appearing on *Top of the Pops* is difficult to beat. But Croke Park came close. They were wonderful experiences – nerve-racking at the time, but also exhilarating. We have toured the UK, Australia, New Zealand, South Africa, America and Canada. There were so many television appearances with so many talented presenters.

And it is still going on. As we sit down to write this final wrap-up we are only days away from a six-week tour of Australia. We will follow this with a month touring Ireland. We might take a few days off then to launch this book!

In September we are going to spend two and a half weeks in Canada. Then we will spend the entire month of November in the UK, travelling the highways and byways on a luxury tour bus. We will do four dates in Ireland after Christmas, then we are off to Scotland in the new year. And so the cycle goes on.

Our latest album, *The Ultimate Collection*, has been doing really well for us. It was a wonderful experience to record, because it was a bit of a departure from the norm. We both recorded duets with people we admired. Scottish legend Jimmy Shand featured on 'The Bluebell Polka' (with Mick), while Daniel O'Donnell and Gloria Hunniford both sang with Tony. Daniel dueted on the old Cliff Richard hit, 'Power to All Our Friends', while Gloria featured on 'True Love'. It brought something new to the double CD set, which also featured some old favourites. Remarkably, it was our thirtieth album to enter the British album charts.

From the start we have been committed recording artists. We have had an album out every year. And we have had an album in the British charts every year. We are very proud of that. The thirty albums we have released in the UK have all been in the British charts. Some have cracked the top twenty, many have been in the top fifty. Thirty years, thirty charting albums: that is an achievement we can look back on with some pride.

We have recorded more than forty albums, but not all have gone on sale in the UK. The albums have also sold well in Australia, New Zealand and South Africa, and have found fans in parts of the USA and Canada too. Our singles have charted at home, in the UK, in Australia, New Zealand and South Africa – reaching number one in some of those territories.

In 2012 Peter Cassidy took over complete management of Foster and Allen. Our years of managing ourselves came to an end. It has worked out great – the Sky 191 programmes, and the TG4 programmes that sprang from them, are a result of Peter's involvement. But one thing has now changed: Peter is acting as our agent and promoter. And he is also handling the UK tour for the first time. We are looking forward to working with him in a new way, and are confident the tour will be as smooth and enjoyable as it always is.

You never rest on your laurels. You are always trying to come up with something else to keep the momentum going. And we hope that soon that momentum may take us to America – on the small screen. We work there with our friend Jim Long and his wife Deborah, who have recently moved to Los Angeles. We are planning with Jim to have our TV series, *The Foster and Allen Show*, broadcast coast to coast in the next year. It will be a new adventure for us.

We don't work as much now as we did a few decades ago. When we began we could do eight weeks without a day off during the summer. Then we became recording artists, and time had to be taken for the albums. The year has gradually settled into a rhythm. That rhythm changes a bit year to year, but we still tour and we will continue to tour. And we still record. That is not going to change any time soon. The tours might be a week or two shorter, and the breaks at home correspondingly longer. But we have no problem with that – time with our families and loved ones is important to both of us.

So this is the end of our book, but it is not the end of our story. That goes on. We hope you have enjoyed this, and if you have, why not stop for a chat after one of our shows? What is music if not a way of sharing the craic?

Tony & Mick

With our friends from over the years at the recording of our 21st anniversary special on *The Gay Byrne Radio Show* at RTÉ.

LEFT TO RIGHT: Seamus Shannon (Shannonside Radio), Moyra Fraser (Foster and Allen Band), Donal Cassidy (Celtic Note Music Store), Aonghus McAnally (producer – *Gay Byrne Radio Show*), Dessie Hynes (Foster and Allen Band), Donie Cassidy (manager/CMR Records), Peter Cassidy (CMR Records), Joe Dolan (international artist), Tony Allen, Frank Sommers (Foster and Allen Band), Tony McNulty (CMR Records), Damien Cassidy (Sky Music), Gordon Smith (Telstar Records UK), Ann Merrigan (CMR Records), Josie Adamson, Derek Hanlon (video producer), Gay Byrne (presenter of *The Gay Byrne Show*), Charlie Landsborough (international singer/songwriter), Brian O'Brien (Telstar Records Ireland), Mick Foster, Mick Clerkin (Ritz Records), Thelma Landsborough, T.R. Dallas (artist and Tony's brother), Ollie Kennedy (Foster and Allen Band), Brian Carty (RTÉ broadcaster).

'Foster & Allen are wonderful ambassadors for Irish Music and are always a joy to see and hear.'

DANIEL O'DONNELL